12612

MEDIEVAL SERBIAN CULTURE

MEDIEVAL SERBIAN CULTURE

Sava Peić

Alpine Fine Arts Collection (UK) Ltd
Publishers of Fine Art Books
London

cover
top left: Stefan Lazarević 'Code of Mining'

top right: The Despot Oliver, Lenovo

bottom left:: The Prophet Elias

bottom right: The Dormition of the Virgin, Sopoćani

back cover:
Angel at Christ's Tomb, Mileševa

Published by
Alpine Fine Arts Collection (UK) Ltd.
43 Manchester Street
London W1M 5PE

Designed by
Paul McTurk BA MCSD

Printed by
Oriental Press, U.A.E.

ISBN 0-88168-263-2

Contents

Acknowledgements

Many individuals and organisations have contributed to this book:

The British Library Board's support has been essential, in allowing me to use the invaluable South-East European Collection. Also the libraries and museums of the former Yugoslavia have been most helpful and supportive.

Many colleagues in Great Britain, former Yugoslavia and America have helped me with their advice, encouragement and their friendship.

I am especially thankful to Jefta Jeftovic, Director of the National Museum in Belgrade, for allowing me to use images from the Museum's collection; to Dr Nada Komnenović, Director of the Fresco Gallery in Belgrade, for her help and advice in the selection of frescoes; to Dušan Milovanović, Custodian of the Museum of Applied Arts in Belgrade; to Rudi Janković, Ray Cassady and, above all, to all my friends for their enduring and constant support in the production of this book.

Special thanks to Mary-Ellen and Gordon Saks, without whose encouragement, in the shadow of the fighting and strife in my country, this book may not have come to fruition.

To the Reader

Notes on the pronunciation of some Serbo-Croat names:

c – (ts) as in 'mats'

ć – (ch) as in 'charge'

č – (soft ch) as in 'arch'

dz – (g) as in 'George'

dj – (soft j) as in 'jive'

j – (y) as in 'yellow'

lj – (li) as in 'life'

nj – (ni) as in 'night'

š – (sh) as in 'shift'

ž – (j) as in French 'jour'

Foreword

This book is written to give the reader, through a chronological approach, a historical perspective of the Serbs, their land and their culture during the Middle Ages. It is divided into: firstly – a brief description and overview of the main events and personalities that shaped medieval Serbian history; followed by a more detailed account of the three most important cultural, artistic and architectural schools from the 9th to 15th centuries; with finally, an epilogue describing Serbia under the Turks.

Each period is defined geographically – as to the various expanding and contracting Serbian empires, with the location of historical landmarks described and illustrated in the text. Each school is sub-divided into Art, Literature and Architecture, and all are described and illustrated within their historical and cultural context.

This book is not intended for the professional scholar, but more for the generally interested reader. Thus the editorial policy has been to exclude footnotes and elaborate cross-references (there is a bibliography at the back for those who wish to research the subject in greater depth), with the main narrative clearly defined, and the more specific descriptions given within the captions.

maps

Introduction

The Serbs come from a special national individuality that belongs to the great family of Slavonic nations. They arrived in the Balkans during the 6th and 7th centuries and occupied the central region of the Balkan Peninsular through which ran the important routes linking Europe with the Middle and Far East.

Ethnographically one nation, the Serbs however were politically divided into a number of independent areas, each with its own ruler, known as the Župan. Two such Serbian states, Raška and Duklja (or Zeta), appeared as early as the late 8th century. In the 12th century, one such Župan, Stefan Nemanja, united all the Serbian states and founded a dynasty that was to rule Serbia for almost 200 years.

Medieval Serbia reached its zenith during the reign of Emperor Dušan, in the middle of the 14th century. After his death the Serbian Empire fell apart. One of the last rulers, Prince Lazar tried to organise a coalition of the Serbs with the Bulgarians, Rumanians, Bosnians and Hungarians, against the spreading Turkish empire. But, in 1389, before he could achieve this, the Turks attacked and defeated the Serbian army on the fields of Kosovo.

The defeated Serbians came under direct rule by Turkey in 1449, and then for over 450 years the entire Serbian nation fell under Turkish domination. A large number of Serbs fled from Turkish reprisals, migrating northwards to Vojvodina and Slavonia.

There was continual armed resistance to the Turks, with two great uprisings in 1804 and 1815. Finally in 1830, the Serbs were accorded the unique status of an autonomous vassal state within the Ottoman Empire. In 1878, at the Berlin Congress, it was recognised as completely independent and four years later the monarchy was reinstated with Prince Milen Obrenović crowned King of Serbia.

By the end of the 19th century Serbia was enjoying a vigorous rate of economic growth, leading to the rise of the bourgeoisie and development of political parties. In 1910 the Balkan states united to drive Turkey out of Macedonia, whose territory was then divided up amongst Serbia, Bulgaria and Greece. In 1913 Bulgaria, dissatisfied with its share of the spoils, turned on its former coalition partner, only to suffer defeat.

In 1914 Serbia was attacked by Austro-Hungarian armies in what became the First World War. Following the general offensive on the Salonika front in Greece, the Serbian army and its allies emerged victorious. Serbia became part of the Kingdom of Serbs, Croats and Slovenes, later in 1929 to be renamed the Kingdom of Yugoslavia.

Peace was not to last when, in 1941, most of Yugoslavia fell under Nazi occupation until the end of the war. Once again, however, their rebellion against the invaders was fierce, and large areas were given up to the partisan resistance. 1945 saw the establishment, under Tito, of the Socialist Federal Republic of Yugoslavia. The constitution gave the Federal Republic of Serbia a smaller area than the Serbia of 1918-29, when Montenegro and the formerly Serbian Macedonia had become separate Republics.

At the time of the 1981 census, the Republic covered an area of some 83,000 square kilometres. It had a population of 9.3 million: 6.2 million of which were Serbs, 1.3 million Albanians, 300.000 ethnic Hungarians, 215,000 Muslims, 150,000 Croats, 150,000 Montenegrans and another 450,000 who simply considered themselves to be Yugoslavs. The main religions being Serbian Orthodox, Muslim and Roman Catholic – all guaranteed equality by the constitution, separated from the state, and with the freedom to perform religious services and rites.

With the break-up of the Eastern Bloc, and the fall of the totalitarian communist system in 1990, Yugoslavia devolved into the independent countries of Croatia, Slovenica, Macedonia, Bosnia and Hercegovina. But, because of political, religious and ethnic differences, the armed struggle for separate national identities returned, and Serbia again became a focus of attention and controversy. In preparing and writing this book, I hope to give some historical perspective to a country in turmoil. To understand the problems of Serbia today, it is necessary to understand its past. In the medieval era Serbia was rich in culture; its literature, art and architecture influenced the world.

Sava Peić, London, July 1994

THE SERBS AND THEIR LANDS

opposite:
6th and 7th centuries – the migrations of nations

The Serbs came initially to the Balkan Peninsula between the 6th and 7th centuries, according to the writings of the Byzantine Emperor and writer, Constantine VII Porphirogenet. They originally settled on the southern coast of the Adriatic and its immediate hinterland. Subsequently they spread through the valley of the river Lim, the river Drina and eventually through the Piva, Tara and Ibar areas. They also settled in the upper reaches of the West Morava river.

The South Slavs came from beyond the Carpathians and settled in parts of the Balkan peninsula and Central Europe during the migration of nations, mostly during the 6th century. They came in groups large and small and in successive waves. The Serbs entered the territories of Byzantium and gradually founded the independent Serbian state. In the Middle Ages, especially from the 12th to the 14th centuries, under the Nemanjić dynasty, Serbia was a powerful state.

Geographically, the areas chosen by the Serbs for their settlements were very well protected, a great advantage militarily in their continuous struggle with other tribes, particularly the Bulgars. It made them a worthwhile and welcome ally for the Byzantines, who were not slow to recognise the implications of the Serbs' growing might. At that time, however, the lands of the Serbs did not form a single state. They were inhabited by tribes led by hereditary princely families, descended from the Župan, who was the head of a tribal state. These were district leaders who were too weak to defend themselves from foreign invaders and were unable to raise their own large armies, but were nevertheless too strong to be forced to become vassals of their brother Serbian Župans.

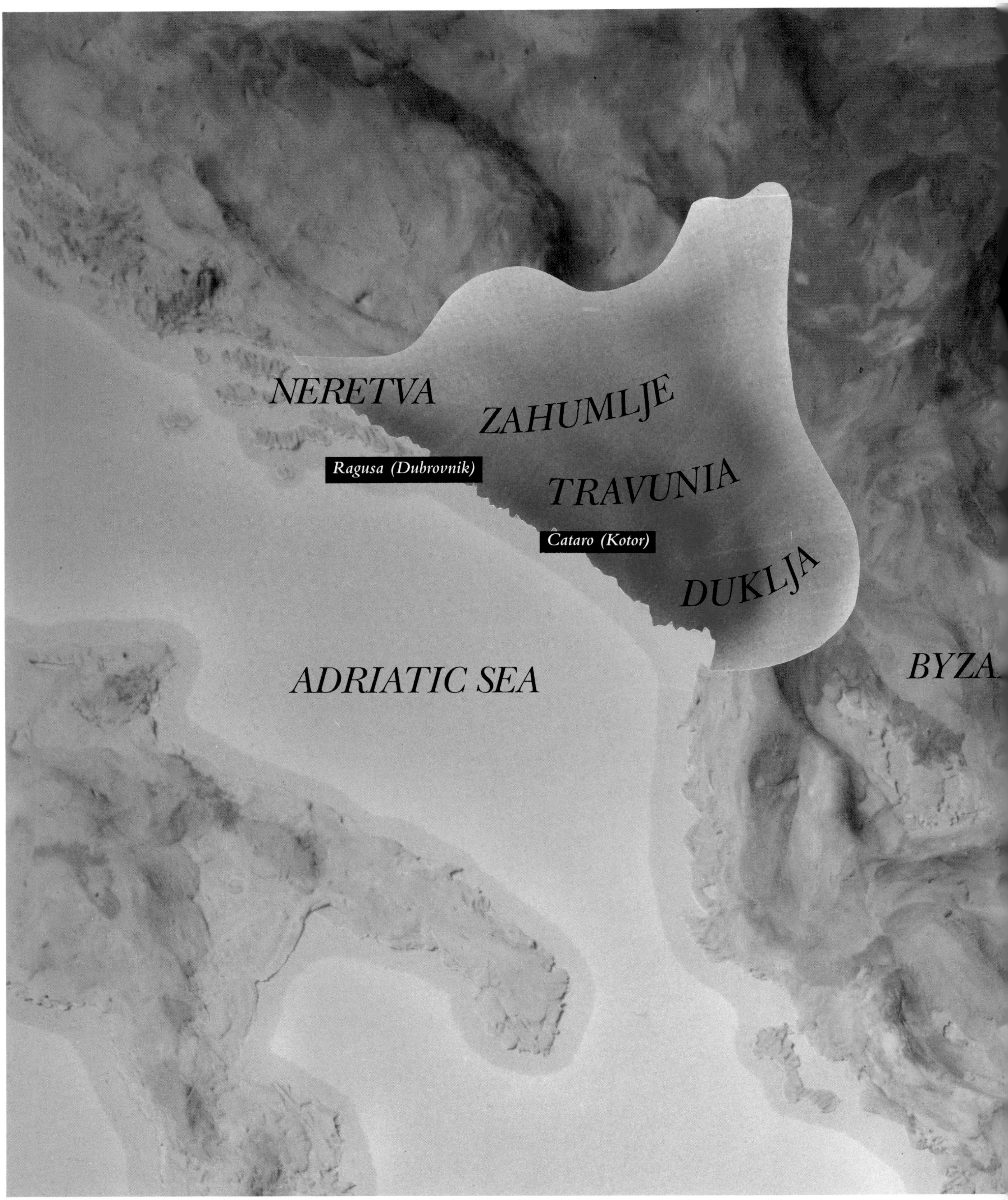

NERETVA

ZAHUMLJE

Ragusa (Dubrovnik)

TRAVUNIA

Cataro (Kotor)

DUKLJA

ADRIATIC SEA

BYZA.

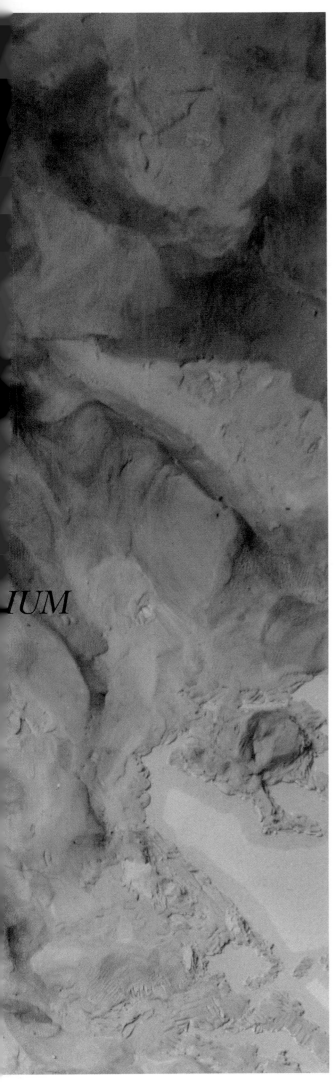

IUM

In the 9th century the Serbs founded their first states in Raška, in the mountains of Serbia and Duklja (Zeta) on the southern coast of the Adriatic. Both these areas backed on to a precarious boundary where the influences of Europe's eastern and western cultures intermingled and confronted each other and where the political interest of the Byzantine empire clashed with those of the Western powers and, more specifically, Rome.

The central part of the Balkans was the place where the eastern and western Roman Empires met and where there was frequent fighting. This was also the area in which Latin and Greek literacy spread most quickly and where Catholicism and Orthodoxy came face to face.

Not much is known about the Serbs' conversion to Christianity, but it probably started between the 7th and 9th centuries, making slow progress initially. This was during the time of the brothers Cyril and Methodius, two monks who were chiefly responsible for the spreading of Christianity among the Slav nation.

Early Literature

Greek and Latin prayer books could not be understood by the Slavs because at that time there was no Slavic alphabet with which to represent their vocal sounds in language. Cyril and Methodius, who came from Salonica and who knew the Slavic language well, devised and originated the characters that formed the Slavic alphabet – called Glagoljica.

It was not until Cyril and Methodius began their work on the translation of missals, gospels, psalters, epistles and rituals from the Greek and Latin rites, and until the introduction of services in the Slavic language known as Old Church Slavic, that the Slavs could understand and appreciate the text of the new faith.

The work of Cyril and Methodius had a significant influence on literacy among the Slavs in the Balkans and they played a prominent role in the pioneering of Christianity among the Slavs, gaining acceptance for their new language; they became universally recognised as the founders of the language of the Church.

In the later part of the 9th century and at the beginning of the 10th, Methodius' disciples were expelled from Moravia for political reasons and they sought asylum in the south, where they found fertile ground for their work among the Macedonians, the Bulgarians and the Serbs. At first they copied Cyril and Methodius' books, preserving the original text. Later they introduced the phonetic, morphological and lexicographic features of their living language into the original text.

above: The two brothers Cyril and Methodius, who knew the Slavic language, devised and originated the characters that formed the alphabet called Glagoljica.

right: The difficult Glagoljica was abandoned for the new Cyrillic alphabet derived by Kliment, the Bishop of Ohrid.

left: St Kliment, a pupil of Cyril and Methodius, came to Ohrid in 886 and inaugurated a period of prolific literature and educational activity.

He introduced the Mass into the Slavic language, had liturgical text translated, and was a teacher of some standing and importance.

The most important changes of that time took place in the east. Cyril's original Slavic alphabet, the difficult Glagolitic, was abandoned for the new Cyrillic and more convenient script derived by Kliment, the Bishop of Ohrid. The Cyrillic script was accepted by all the Slavs of the orthodox denomination, and, in a modified form, is still used today by all Bulgarians, Russians, Macedonians and Serbs.

In 891, during the reign of the Serbian Crown Prince Mutimir, the Serbian bishopric came into being, but the destiny of the new religion seemed even at that time to be doubtful. The problem was whether the new Serbian Church would ultimately fall under the Roman or the Byzantine influence.

During the next few centuries Serbia and its people attracted a great deal of hostility and the Serbs were victims of the struggles between Rome and Constantinople. It was at this time that they were converted to the Roman rite by Roman clerics, whilst the Byzantine church was pre-occupied by internal theological disputes and struggles. The Serbs were finally won over to the Orthodox church during the reign of Stefan Nemanja and his family, who were the founders of both the Serbian state and the Serbian church.

King Stefan Nemanja (The Grand Župan), founder of the Nemanjić Dynasty

The Nemanjić Dynasty

With the strengthening of this long-established dynasty at the end of the 12th century, art really blossomed. This was at a time when Byzantine political and cultural influence had begun to wane after conditions facilitated the development of national schools in Serbia. The heads of the Serbian state from the 12th to the 14th centuries were, with their families, the founders of the new Serbian art and among other associated Serbian dignitaries, there were a lot of individuals who were literally gifted and inclined towards art. Their participation manifested itself firstly in the choice of the artists, who came from the best workshops of Constantinople and Salonica, and secondly in the creation of regional historical and religious frescoes, well represented in the general iconography of the Serbian Christian church.

They built monasteries and churches primarily as mausoleums or royal burial chambers. They erected towns and military fortifications, commissioned frescoes and icons and promoted the copying of books and illuminating of manuscripts. These Serbian rulers spent most of their considerable wealth (mainly derived from gold and silver mines in the Serbian mountains) on these activities and they spared no expense in building and decorating their churches, lavishly decorating them with wall paintings and portraits of the founders, the highest ecclesiastic dignitaries, archbishops, royal councils and coronations, the genealogical tree of the Nemanjić dynasty, representations of their deaths and the re-internment of their relics, all were themes for Serbian iconography. Some of these icons and frescoes are among the finest wall paintings produced anywhere in medieval Europe.

1350

Tsar Uroš V
1355-1371
(The last Tsar of Serbia)

King Uroš IV Dušan
1331-1355
(crowned Tsar of Serbia and Greece in 1346)

King Uroš III Dečanski
1321-1331
(overthrown and imprisoned by his son)

1300

King Uroš II Milutin
1282-1321
(Serbia's greatest patron to the Arts and Architecture)

King Dragutin
1276-1282
(abdicated in favour of his brother Milutin)

King Uroš I
1243-1276
(overthrown by by his son and became a monk)

1250

Queen Jelena
(great benefactor to the Orthodox Church)

King Radoslav
1228-1234
(overthrown by feudal lords)

King Vladislav
1234-1243
(overthrown by feudal lords)

1200

Rastko (St Sava)
(became the monk Sava in 1192)
The First Archbishop of the
Serbian Orthodox Church in 1219

Stefan Nemanja
The Grand Zupan 1170-1196
(abdicated and become the monk Simon)

Stefan Provenčani
The First Crowned 1196-1228
(established the Serbian Orthodox Church in 1219)

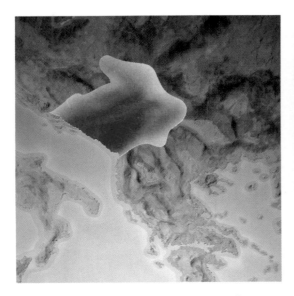

Serbia under Stephan Nemanja (The Grand Župan)

Shortly after Nemanja's death, fragrant oil began to flow from his body, which was found to have miracle-working powers, and Stefan Nemanja was canonised, becoming known as Saint Simeon.

Stefan Nemanja (1114–1200)

Stefan Nemanja was born in Ribnica (Zeta) and was baptised by Latin priests. On his arrival at Ras he was again baptised by an Orthodox priest, in the church of St Peter and Paul. His name is first mentioned during the Hungarian-Byzantine struggles. Towards the end of the 12th century he united Raška and Duklja (Zeta) and formed the first great Serbian state, which he ruled from 1170 to 1196. He came to power after the death of the mighty Byzantine Emperor, Manuel Comnenus, after liberating the Serbian lands from Byzantine rule. During his reign, Nemanja generously assisted the clergy and left behind large endowments to the church. His reign ended when he abdicated in favour of his son Stefan and took up the monastic life, choosing the name Simeon.

Nemanja was not only an able military leader and administrator, but a man of deep piety. His monastic life was first spent in Studenica and later at Mount Athos. Shortly after his death he was canonised and proclaimed as being of Svetorodni (born of holy stock).

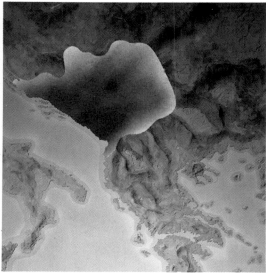

Serbia under Stefan 'The First Crowned'

Stefan Prvovenčani, the First Crowned (1196-1228)

Nemanja's son Stefan Prvovenčani, the first crowned, inherited and expanded the realm in which the ruler's power was strengthened. After the Crusaders conquered Constantinople and overthrew the Emperor, the situation changed dramatically. Stefan turned towards the west and received the King's crown from the Pope (in 1217), which is why he is known as Stefan Prvovenčani, Stefan the First Crowned.

One of his main achievements was the establishment of an independent archbishopric in Serbia, with the help of his youngest brother, Sava, later St. Sava. The King's brother Sava, a monk on Mount Athos (the Holy Mountain) returned to Serbia and undertook a diplomatic mission to Nicaea, the centre of Greek Asia Minor. The Nicæans were fighting for the restoration of the Byzantine empire, its laws and traditions. In 1219, Sava succeeded in persuading the emperor and Patriarch to allow him to form the Serbian archbishopric and he became its first archbishop. The first archbishopric was established at a place called Žiča, where Stefan founded a monastery.

St Sava (1174–1236)

St Sava, the first archbishop of the independent Serbian Orthodox church, was the youngest son of Stefan, the Grand Župan of Serbia. When he was 18 he went secretly to Mount Athos, where, in spite of his father's wishes, he became the monk Sava. In 1196 his father abdicated and, like his son, he too took up the religious life and became a monk known as Simeon, on Mount Athos.

Together father and son founded the monastery at Hilandar, which became the great centre of Serbian theological learning. Later, as archbishop, he set himself the task of securing the independence of the Serbian church to promote education and introduce ecclesiastical reforms. The first written work of St Sava is popularly considered to mark the beginning of Serbian literature.

King Radoslav (1228-1234)

After the death of the first Serbian king, Stefan Prvovenčani "the First Crowned" in 1228, his elder son Radoslav succeeded him to the throne, in accordance with the explicit wish of his father. Radoslav (1228-1234) was married to the daughter of John I Angelus, the governor of Epirus, and policy under the new king moved the country's political leanings from the west to the east.

The Serbian landed gentry could not accept King Radoslav's Byzantine policy and the discontent of the Serbian feudal lords culminated in the overthrow of Radoslav who was replaced by Stefan's younger son Vladislav.

King Vladislav (1234–1243)

The reign of Vladislav lasted ten years. This change in the Serbian succession also affected the country's external policy. King Vladislav was supported by Bulgaria and married a Bulgarian princess, the daughter of John Asan II.

During Vladislav's reign St Sava left his position as Serbian archbishop and retired at the Assembly in Žiča. Soon after this, he set out for the east, visiting Palestine, Alexandria and Nicaea. On his return he became ill and died in Tirnovo (Bulgaria) on 14 January 1236. King Vladislav brought Sava's remains back to Serbia and buried them in the royal monastery of Mileševa.

Once again the Serbian landed gentry were dissatisfied with the king. They rose against Vladislav, dethroned him and brought the third son of Stefan "the First Crowned", Uroš I, to the throne in 1243.

King Stefan Uroš I (1243-1276)

Uroš ruled the Kingdom of Serbia for over thirty years. He kept a close eye on the situation in the Balkans. Byzantium was restored in 1261 and Hungary began to grow rapidly into a first-rate power. Serbia started to feel pressurised from the north and south. Frequent and bitter battles were fought during the reign of King Uroš and these were to establish the shape and frontiers of the Serbian state. Uroš carried out a policy of reconciliation with his neighbours. The expansion of mining helped him to strengthen Serbia and also to maintain good relations with church dignitaries, both Catholic and Orthodox. Many of the personalities who attended his court had a great influence on medieval policy. Prominent in this were his wife Queen Jelena, who came from the French royal family of Anjou; his mother, Anna, who was a member of a Venetian ducal family Dandoli; and the Hungarian-born wife of his elder son Dragutin, Katalina, who also lived at his court. The Serbian environment was naturally vastly influenced by the trends of western culture. In keeping with the custom of previous Serbian medieval rulers, Uroš also built a monastery school, at Sopoćani. The principal reason for building this monastery was to atone for his sins.

17

Queen Jelena

Queen Jelena was a Frenchwoman from the House of Anjou. She was a Catholic and had a Latin education. She shared in all King Uroš' important political decisions. The Pope considered her a true daughter of the Catholic Church.

During her husband's lifetime she showed herself to be a patron of the Orthodox Church; she built the monastery at Gradac. After her husband's death she began to support the Catholic Church in that part of the coastal region and she governed it until her death.

King Stefan Dragutin (1276–1282)

Uroš was dethroned by his son Dragutin, who deeply resented the fact that his father distrusted him. Dragutin persistently demanded to rule part of the Serbian region and warred against his father, overthrowing him and becoming King of Serbia himself in 1276. Uroš became a monk and died the following year.

King Dragutin did not hold power for long. He was unfortunate enough to fall off his horse and became a cripple. Discouraged both physically and morally, he soon gave up the throne in favour of his younger brother, Milutin. From the very beginning, the two were in conflict, but they were reconciled in 1313 and thereafter acted together. Dragutin died shortly afterwards, leaving his kingdom to his son Vladislav.

Vladislav however, did not receive his inheritance. He was immediatly imprisoned by his uncle, Milutin, but escaped to Hungary and subsequently disappeared.

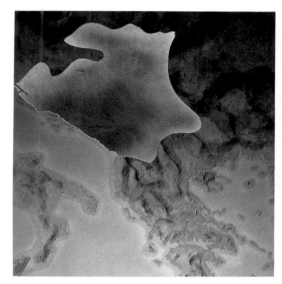

Serbia under King Milutin

King Stefan Uroš II Milutin (1282–1321)

The next important Serbian ruler was Milutin (1281–1321). During his reign Serbian territory was extended southwards at the expense of Byzantine Macedonia. The Byzantine emperor Andronicus II, was too weak to resist Serbian expansion and had no other option but to accept it. Milutin was prepared to maintain friendly relations with the emperor evidenced by his marriage to the emperor's daughter.

Serbia prospered during the reign of King Milutin. There was silver and gold mining; commerce and crafts flourished; agriculture and farming brought in good incomes. Everything that came from either east or west was eagerly accepted and adopted, changed and added to. The most important legacies from the long reign of King Milutin are the many endowments he made and the churches he erected. No other king of the Nemanjić dynasty left such a rich architectural and artistic heritage as Milutin.

King Stefan Uroš III Dečanski (1321–1331)

Milutin's death in 1321 was followed by bitter quarrels over who would succeed him. The eventual victor was Stefan, known as Stefan Dečanski, after the monastery he founded at Dečani. During his father's life Stefan Dečanski had been blinded for attempted rebellion. In spite of this he was able to establish his claim to his father's throne. During his reign the Serbian kingdom was further extended into Macedonia where Serbia and Bulgaria were rivals. Not long afterwards Stefan Dečanski was dethroned and imprisoned by his son Dušan, and eventually strangled.

map of Serbia during the reign of King Uroš IV Dušan

King Stefan Uroš IV Dušan (1331-1355)

Under Tsar Dušan, medieval Serbia reached the zenith of its power. He was crowned Tsar (Emperor) of the Serbs and Greeks in Skopje in 1346. Several campaigns of conquest, mainly directed southwards at Byzantine territory, extended the borders of Dušan's Macedonia and Albania as far as Thessaly and Epirus.

This made the Serbian state the leading power in the Balkans and Dušan was obliged to dedicate most of his energy to the preservation of his enormous realm, which stretched from the Sava and the Danube in the north to the Gulf of Corinth in the south. Dušan never achieved his ultimate ambition of taking over Byzantium. He was succeeded by his son Stefan Uroš V and after his death his empire quickly disintegrated.

Tsar Stefan Uroš V (1355–1371)

Stefan Uroš was unable to hold the Serbs together: the lords of the various provinces grew much stronger and eventually became independent feudal lords. Simultaneously with the weakening of the Serbian state, the Turks gained in military might. Having already created bases for themselves on European soil, they now launched a campaign of conquest. Instead of battering against a single powerful state, the Turks were only met by token resistance from the disunited, quarrelling feudal lords. After the Battle of Marica in 1371 and the death of Stefan Uroš, the last Serbian tsar, the Nemanjić family dynasty came to an end. Many of Serbia's nobles accepted the Turkish yoke and became vassals of the Sultan. One of the most famous of these was Prince Marko, the ruler of Prilep. As the legendary Prince Marko, he became a hero whose adventures form the theme of a cycle of songs from Serbian national poetry.

Prince Lazar Hrebeljanović (1371-1389)

After King Uroš V, the feudal lords broke away from the weakening Serbian state and moved northwards to the region of Prince Lazar Hrebeljanović, who imposed himself on the other lords and proclaimed himself Nemanja's successor. Apart from Lazar, there were other prominent Serbian lords whom Prince Lazar had neither the strength nor the time to subjugate and thus unite the Serbian state.

All his efforts at statehood were thwarted by the Turks. They raided Lazar's region for the first time in 1381 and warned him that the time for decisive battle was imminent. Preparation took a long time on both sides and it was decided that the site should be the Plain of Kosovo. The battle began on St Vitus' day, Tuesday 15 June 1389. In the early stages of the battle Prince Lazar did have some small successes, but after several hours of fighting his army was routed. Both armies suffered heavy losses and both commanders, Prince Lazar and the Sultan Murat I, were killed.

Prince Lazar was caught by the Turks, according to the writings of Constantine the Philosopher, and beheaded. "Lazar met his death in holy bliss, while his beloved companions prayed with all their hearts to be killed before, not to see his own death."

The Battle of Kosovo

The Turks raided Lazar's region for the first time in 1381 and warned Prince Lazar that the time for a decisive battle was imminent. Preparation for the battle took a long time on both sides. The two armies met on St Vitus' day 15 June 1389. In the beginning the Serbs had the advantage, particularly after Sultan Murat was assassinated by a Serb named Miloš Obilić. His younger son, Bayazit, ordered that the Sultan's death be concealed, killed his brother Jacob, called all the Turkish forces together, made the decisive charge and reversed the situation on the field. He took Prince Lazar prisoner and killed him immediately. The death of Sultan Murat and the fact that the Turks withdrew immediately created the impression that the Serbs had won the battle and Europe rejoiced in the Christian victory.

Unfortunately the ruling Prince and the dukes and nobles of Serbia, as well as thousands of their soldiers, were killed in the heroic attempt to preserve their freedom and protect the European Christian civilisation.

The battle of Kosovo was the inevitable clash of two worlds; the Christian and the Islamic. It has become one of the great paradoxes of history: although it was a Turkish victory, and marked the first stage in their eventual conquest of the medieval Serbian kingdom, in the folk memory of the Serbs, this military defeat was transmitted into a spiritual victory and regarded as a source of pride rather than humiliation. Prince Lazar and Miloš later became cult figures of the Kosovo legend.

Besides that of Christ, no other name is more beautiful or more sacred to the Serbs than Kosovo.

Both represent drama and sacrifice. Christ is a dramatic sacrifice for all of mankind, while Kosovo was the cause of both great suffering and great pride to the Serbian people - a profound tragedy written in blood.

Despot Stefan Lazarević (1389-1427)

Prince Lazar's successor, his son, Despot Stefan Lazarević, retreated before the Turks and, with the help of his mother, Princess Milica, strove hard to establish order in his new principality around the Morava river, and to save the remains of the Serbian state. He achieved what appeared to be an impossible task and gained international prestige. He was a Turkish vassal and Hungarian Palatine (from 1402). He worked for good relations within the principality, founded and improved the central administration which gave him control over the subordinated nobility and built new fortifications, monasteries (Resava) and churches. He was a patron of the arts and a man of letters, the last representative of the dying era of the knights and also a herald of the new Renaissance period. His principality became a refuge for the most eminent men of letters, scholars, monks and feudal lords, who, having lost their own lands, brought with them the best of Byzantine, Bulgarian and one-time Serbian traditions. The period of the Serbian despotate under Stefan Lazarević created its own atmosphere, a kind of sunset splendour increasingly overshadowed by the doom of extinction.

After the fall of Serbia, the Serbian state was divided into Ottoman administration units: sanjaks, kadiliks and nahijas. The Serbian ruling class, the feudal lords, mostly fled the country or were killed, though there was a minority who agreed to co-operate with the Turks. The lands and the incomes of the previous rulers fell into the Sultan's hands and the property of the feudal lords was divided into timars (Turkish feudal estates) and given to the spahis (Turkish warriors). This Turkish conquest was followed by large-scale movements of the Serbian population. Thousands of fugitives fled to Hungarian territory, where the population had been decimated by Turkish attacks. The social and political life of the Serbs was maintained to a certain extent among these refugees in Hungary.

In the renewed campaign under Suleman the Magnificent (1520-1566) the territory of present Vojvodina also fell to the Turks. The frontiers moved far to the north and west, with the Serbian population moving in front of them. Within a century the Serbs found themselves scattered over large areas far from their homeland. They reached Dalmatia, Croatia, Slavonia and distant parts of Hungary. The Hapsburg rulers of the remaining Croatian and Hungarian lands systematically settled Serbs there as protection against Ottoman incursions.

left: the fortified capital at Smederevo

Despot Georgy Branković (1427-1456)

In 1427 Stefan Lazarević was succeeded by his nephew, Georgy Branković, who from the beginning faced troubles from which he was to have little respite throughout his long reign. Most of this time he was a despot without a despotate, wandering through neighbouring states seeking help to restore his shattered kingdom.

He was forced to surrender Belgrade to Hungary and Niš and Kruševac to the Turks. To defend himself and the Serbs, he built a new fortified capital at Smederevo. For some years a precarious peace was maintained with the Turks, but in 1428 the Sultan began a new campaign against Hungary, in the course of which Smederevo was captured and Serbia cruelly plundered; the despot lost his estates in Hungary. Not long before his death he was forced to sign a treaty with the Sultan which left him only a small territory north of the western Morava. In 1456 he died, his little state by then beset by a bitter succession of quarrels. The Sultan took advantage of this situation and captured Smederevo in 1459. Serbia from that time ceased to exist as a political power.

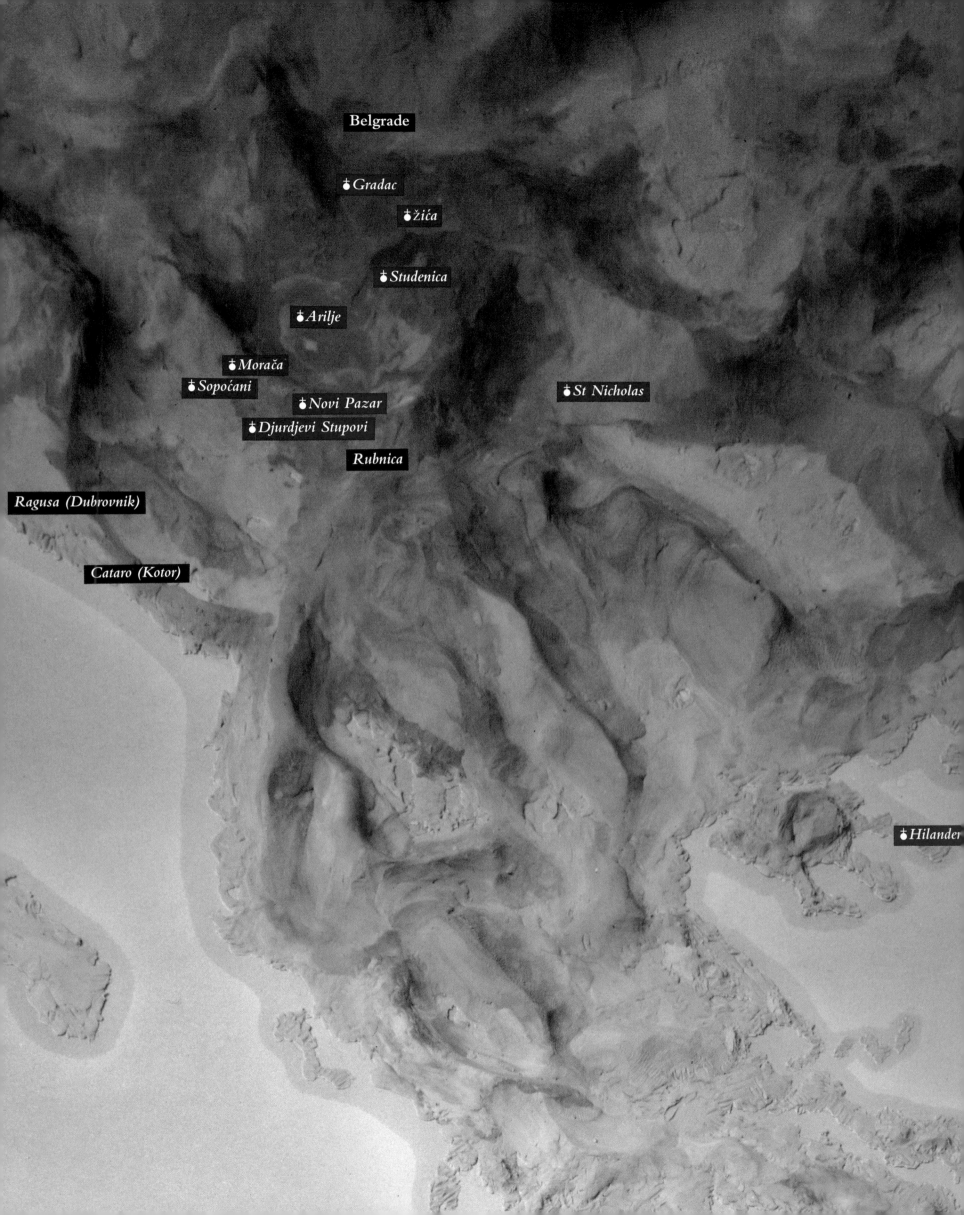

Chapter Two

THE RAŠKA SCHOOL

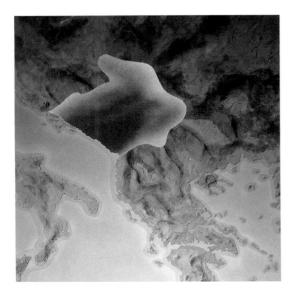

Serbia under Stefan Nemanja (The Grand Župan)

In the 9th century, the Serbs established their first states in the mountains of Serbia and Zeta on the southern coastline of the Adriatic. Both states were on the crossroads between east and west and the exchanging of ideas fostered the creation of an interesting cultural and artistic symbiosis. These exceptional circumstances greatly influenced the fate and development of Serbian art.

Stylistic wavering and the unequal value of the first period of old Serbian art were the direct result of the clear political and cultural commitment of the two states. Raška turned towards Byzantium, because the Byzantine church had an advantage over the Roman Catholic church; the Byzantine church allowed the founding of independent national ecclesiastical organisations in which liturgical services could be conducted in the countries' own language. This gave a genuine stimulus to the Serbs for learning and for the creation of a national literature and the translation of works from other languages.

Unfortunately, Raška has no extant significant historical monuments from the acceptance of Christianity and the establishment of the states of the Nemanjić dynasty. A unique example of this era is the church of St Peter, near Novi Pazar, with its badly faded and nearly unrecognisable fresco in the dome. Whereas the other state, Zeta, has characteristics of the early Romanesque period, Latin in style, it had its own architecture, sculpture, murals and paintings.

Towards the end of the 12th century, when this politically and economically independent state was established under the rule of the Grand Župan, Stefan Nemanja, it was he who united Raška and Duklja. When his younger son Sava founded the independent church in 1219, all these cultural bridges connected Serbia to the best known centres of world art, Constantinople and Salonica on the one hand and the Adriatic coast and Venice on the other.

The unification of Raška and Duklja linked specific features of the medieval art of Serbia - Latin rationalism and Greek mysticism – so that Maniera Graeca and Maniera Latina merged into Serbia. This is demonstrated through the unique artistic expression of builders, sculptors, painters and craftsmen, which produced a symbiosis which did not clash with the heterogeneous elements and as a result is a synthesis which defines Serbian art as original and autochthonous.

Literature

S ava organised the life of the Serbian church and was the initiator of most of the intense literary works of the Serbs, from the most learned monks starting to copy pious books, the majority of which have not survived: an exception is the famous 12th century Gospel of Prince Miroslav, a monumental and richly illuminated manuscript written in about 1185, which is famous for its lettering and beautiful miniatures.

Miròslav's gospel

Miroslav's gospel was written and illuminated in the 1180's for Prince Miroslav of Hum, brother of the Serbian Grand Župan Stefan Nemanja. It was named after the prince, who had probably commissioned the manuscript for the church of St Peter, and is the oldest preserved Serbian Cyrillic manuscript.

On the last leaf, the scribe Gligorije describes how this important volume came into existence, how he illuminated the gospel in gold for Prince Miroslav and how he prayed that God would keep and protect him, the scribe. The lettering and illuminations indicate that Gligorije was not the only author of this book. The high level of development and the great beauty of the letters and painted initials show that Hum must have had a literary and scribal school which cultivated a sophisticated art of writing and painting even before Miroslav's gospel, using Slavonic translation of the original Greek text with elements of the new, Serbian version.

The elaborate initials and headpieces in the gospel are beautifully drawn, lavishly coloured, decorated with gold leaf; they are particularly important features of this exceptional manuscript. Its parchment leaves contain 296 miniatures and embellished initials.

The text was written by quill pen dipped in black ink and is laid out in columns. Red ink was used for most of the headings. The miniatures and initials were first drawn with a pen and then painted with a brush. The large initials are a combination of geometric and vegetal motifs and the most beautiful are those containing animals and human figures.

The animals are usually the eagle, egret, peacock, snake and fish, wolf, dog, panther and lion. The human figures are usually four Evangelists, who were painted several times and in different ways, as well as Christ, John the Baptist and others.

*above/opposite: Miroslav's Gospel
(National Museum, Belgrade)*

СЮ · А · Н
П
ЬШ · КЬ
ПЕСLN
ТААНА
МЕКА
ЧХЮСС

ТЫБЫГАСЬПОМН СТ НАСТННЕ ПРНЗДЕ ШН
СІСОННЕ СЛОВОЙСЛО ЛІСТВОУЕТВОСВЕТЙ Н
ВОВЕ ШЕ БА Н СВЕТ АСТ НЕ ІНН ЙЖ
ВЕВЕ СЛОВО ЙСЕВЕН ПРОСВЕЩАЕТВСАКОГОУ
СІСОНІ ШВБ АЙВСАТ М ГРЕДОУ ЩА ТОВ МНРЕ ВЫ

The paintings of Miroslav's gospels served as models
for miniature paintings in Serbia and Bosnia in the
13th, 14th and 15th centuries.

33

Some of the most flowery literature of the Middle Ages was that of the Serbs. Serbian literature began to develop as a result of the strengthening of the Serbian state. The beginning of this Serbian literacy was started by Sava, the youngest brother of Stefan "the First Crowned", when he won autonomy for the Serbian Orthodox Church.

The end of the 12th century saw the beginning of the Serbian national culture, when the Raška school of Serbian art was formed. It was most evident in the first written Serbian biographies. At the beginning of the 13th century, Sava wrote a biography of his father called Office for St Simeon and this work marks the real beginning of the original Serbian literature. Sava was not a professional writer, he was a religious man, an organiser of the church and state. He wrote a number of manuscripts on the organisation of monasteries in Serbia. His biography of his father was part of the Typicon for Studenica monastery.

John of Damascus wrote the famous novel of Barlaam and Joasaph, one of the most read and translated works of the Middle Ages. The young Indian prince Joasaph, on the advice of the wise man Barlaam, renounced worldly riches to devote himself to moral virtues and higher ideals. In Serbia, this hero was compared to Prince Rasko, the youngest son of Stefan Nemanja, later St Sava, who adopted a similar course. Sava himself may have selected the text on the scroll of Prince Joasaph: "My son, Joasaph, leave the transitory kingdom and taking up the cross, follow Christ".

In 1216 Stefan "the First Crowned" wrote the whole life-story of his father, Stefan Nemanja, from his birth to his death. In the 13th century a monk from Mount Athos, Domentian, described the lives of the Grand Župan Stefan Nemanja (St Simeon) and Sava (St Sava) at great length and with many elaborations.

Teodosije, another monk from Mount Athos, subsequently revised both biographies and purged them of their excesses of pathos and rhetoric.

Hagiographies, a genre inherited from Byzantine literature, were very popular, but those written by the Serbian authors differed in style from the originals. The Serbian biographies were more understandable when they were studied in context side by side with Serbian architecture, paintings and mosaics.

left: Barlaam and Joasaph are depicted in the lowest zone among the saints in the church of the Virgin Mary, Studenica

Architecture

Serbian architecture experienced its first bloom in the second half of the 12th century, during the reign of Grand Župan Stefan Nemanja. In this significant period of Serbian medieval architecture the kings and feudal lords vied with one another to build churches, mausoleums and monasteries as their personal manifestations. Several stylistic currents and schools developed during this period. The fundamental type of church construction adopted during the 13th and 14th centuries belonged to the so-called Raška school. These churches had a single nave surmounted by a cupola and proceeded by a natherex placed under the same roof. Some had one or two tower belfries facing west.

The apse of the alter was semi-circular. The walls were usually of stone, but the facades of the plainer structures were covered with parget and those of the more elaborate ones covered in polished marble. Under the edges of the roof there were often arcature friezes over consoles. Their portals and windows showed traces of Romanesque style, which had reached Raška from the Adriatic. Important features of Serbian churches and mausoleums were the ornamental sculptures which were unpopular in the Byzantine Orthodox world. These sculptures represented fantastic religious figures combined with typical floral ornaments.

The rulers of the Nemanjić dynasty often engaged architects and masons from the coastal areas of the Adriatic to build their churches, and Greek painters, usually from Constantinople or Salonica, to paint their frescoes.

By combining these architectural and painting styles in this way, a new type of church building, known as a Raška church, emerged from the Byzantine idea of the temple. The Romanesque style of building and eastern iconography are demonstrated in the architectural style of churches and chapels.

The most important monasteries belonging to this stylistic group are the churches of St Nicholas, Djurdjevi Stupovi, Studenica, Žiča Mileševa, Morača, Sopoćani and Arilje. All these edifices have lateral parclisses (small chapels with domes).

Churches and Monasteries

Monastic life was well established in the Byzantine empire, and there were many famous monasteries in Constantinople and elsewhere. There were no monasteries in Serbia until the Serbs became politically independent of the empire. During the reign of the Grand Župan Stefan Nemanja, in the late 12th century, Serbia achieved its independence. Most of the famous Serbian monasteries were built by Nemanja and his successors, who became the royal dynasty of Serbia for the next 200 years. These monasteries were built as mausoleums or royal burial places. They are now the only existing Serbian treasure houses; they are fascinating for their noble exteriors, and the wealth of their treasures, icons and frescoes of the saints, their gold and silver wrought by master-craftsmen and books written by self-sacrificing monks.

Church of St Peter and Paul

*One of the oldest religious edifices in Serbia.
Stefan Nemanja's biographers: his son King Stefan
"the First Crowned" and St Sava, said that it was in
St Peter's that Nemanja converted from the Catholic to
the Orthodox church and convened a council
condemning the Bogomils.*

*It was in St Peter's that Stefan Nemanja abdicated
in favour of his son. It was also the seat of the Raška
bishopric and metropolitan.*

*St Peter's is a small early Romanesque rotunda built
of stone, with an inscribed cross, and surmounted by a
great dome with four windows. Inside the church the
dome rests on four massive pilasters.*

Djurdjevi Stupovi

The monastery of St George was commissioned by
Stefan Nemanja. This is an unusual monastery
surrounded by massive walls. The central part of the
fortification is occupied by the church, with other
buildings encircling it. It was built on a narrow area
and the monastery complex resembles a small citadel
with closely surrounded buildings.

King Dragutin, following his abdication in favour of
his brother, King Milutin, transformed the original
main entrance of the monastery fortification into a
chapel. He was buried in the monastery in 1316.

The monastery fresco paintings have not survived;
only the monumental figure of St George on a white
horse and badly damaged frescoes of excerpts from his
life still exist. These are supreme achievements of late
12th century painting in Serbia.

Studenica Monastery

*The oldest church in the monastery of Studenica is
dedicated to the Virgin and was built between 1183
and 1196. Its founder was Stefan Nemanja, who took
his monastic orders in this church and is buried here,
his relics having been brought from Hilandar in 1208
or 1209. The church's form is a single nave building
with a dome. On the eastern side is a tripartite
sanctuary, on the western side a narthex and two
lateral vestibules comprise the north and south sides.
The dome rests on the cubic base. It is twelve-sided,
built of brick and decorated from outside with niches
and arcades supported on semi-columns. The facade is
made of blocks of polished marble. One, two and three-
light windows are harmoniously arranged on the facade.
The richly carved decoration, with
copious sculptures in the Roman style, emphasise the
Romanesque character of the building.*

Studenica – *The church of the Virgin Mary*

left: The central church of Studenica, is one of the most beautiful and splendid architectural monuments of medieval Serbia. It was built by Stefan Nemanja after he had united the country.

Nemanja's youngest son, Sava, the first archbishop of the independent Serbian church and a writer, refers to the building at Studenica in his Life of Nemanja.

The ground on which the church was built was originally a deserted hunting-ground for wild beasts. When the lord and ruler, Stefan Nemanja, who was king of all Serbia, came to hunt there, it pleased him so much that he built a monastery in this secluded place.

Stefan Nemanja endowed the monastery with icons, church vessels, books, vestments and hanging tapestries. All these were recorded in the monastery's charter and on a wall in the church.

This church, Nemanja's most important foundation, served also as the mausoleum of his dynasty during the first decades of their rule.

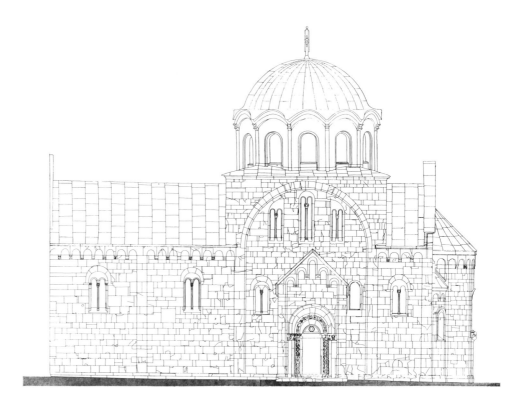

below: ***Studenica –*** *Chapel of King Radoslav, son of Stefan Prvovenčani"the First Crowned" 1234*

Studenica – *The church of the Virgin Mary*

above: The position of Christian churches is traditionally with the altar facing east. The sunrise is significant for the Orthodox religion and means "The Christ is light of the world, the light of Truth".

right: Ground plan

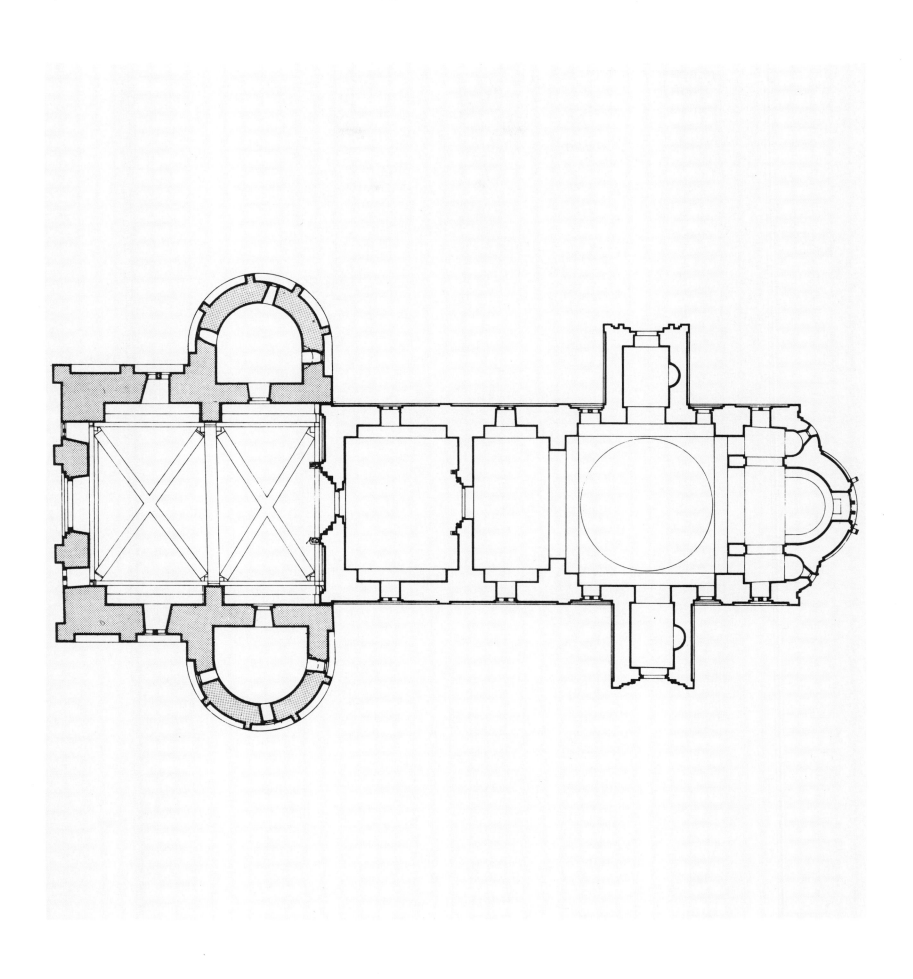

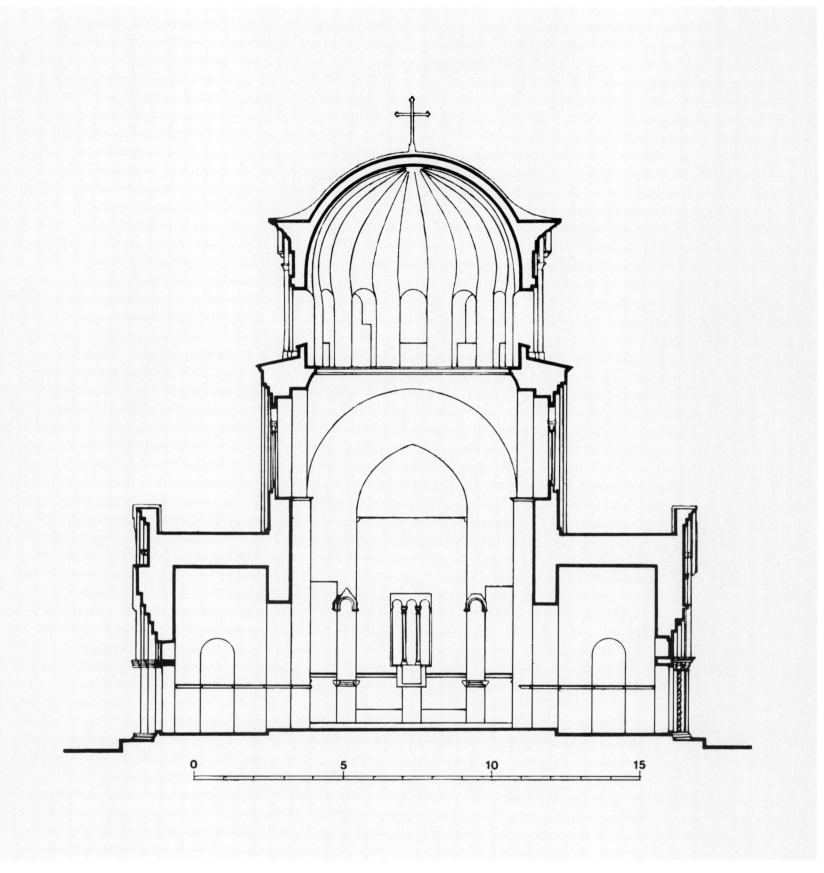

Studenica - *Church of the Virgin Mary*
above: Cross-section
right: Longitudinal section

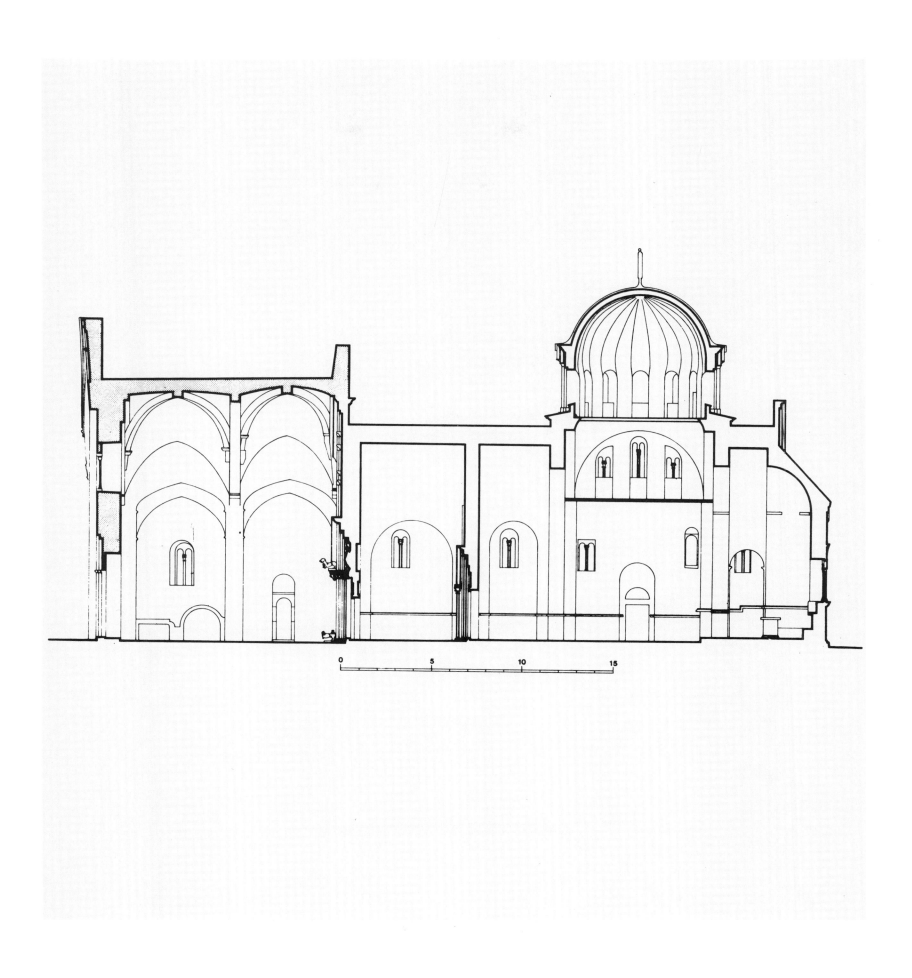

Studenica - *Church of the Virgin Mary*
above: King Radoslav's narthex (cross-section)

King Radoslav, Nemanja's grandson built a large narthex in the 1330's. Studenica was built to serve as a mausoleum for the Great Župan Nemanja and his wife Anna. His elder son, King Stefan "the First Crowned", King Radoslav and the Great Duke Vukan are also buried there.

right: Three-light window of the altar apse. Animals and plants were often ascribed certain characteristics and were used to symbolise people who possessed such qualities as, for example, the eagle, the siren and the serpent etc.

Studenica - *Church of the Virgin Mary
(The West portal)*

*above and right: The tympanum contains a carving of
the Virgin with the baby on her lap surrounded by the
archangels Michael and Gabriel, bowing towards the
new-born Messiah-Christ. This scene is widespread
and represents the cult of "Mother of God" and many
churches in Serbia were dedicated to her.*

Studenica - *Church of the Virgin Mary*
(The West portal)

*left: Siren, relief on the left side of the outer frame of
the three-light window*

*right: Lamb with a cross, relief on the left side of the
outer frame of the three-light window*

Studenica - *Church of the Virgin Mary*
(The West portal)

left: The eagle and the siren below the right hand of the Virgin are symbols of earthly paradise. Nemanja and Sava are compared with eagles soaring to the heavenly heights.

below: Three-light window with part of the facade of the church of the Virgin Mary. The high level of craftsmanship at Studenica is particularly notable in the more complex parts of the building: the windows, portals and carved ornamentation.

Studenica - Church of the Virgin Mary

right: The figure of Christ carved on the underside of the lintel which symbolically means "the Heavenly King". The sculpture of Studenica originated in an area in which Byzantine and Romanesque ideas intermingled. Basically, sculptures were executed within a Romanesque frame, though they contain elements of Byzantine stone reliefs.

Studenica - Church of the Mother of God

far right: A view of the eastern part of the altar in the Church of the Mother of God in Studenica, with its magnificent iconostasis, gives an impression of the interior of Orthodox temples which, in the 13th century, represented the ideal precondition for creating monumental art, with their unique space, good lighting and large, flat walls.

Paintings

Serbian painting of the 13th century is characterised by its specific representative quality and monumentality. All monasteries have unique styles of fresco paintings. In the beginning, Serbian art, for example the fresco painting, kept well within the framework of the Byzantine tradition, using the specific fresco technique of painting, i.e. applying paint directly on to a fresh, damp wall. The colour reacted chemically with the upper layer of plaster, sinking into and combining with it. This helped to keep the colours of frescoes unchanged throughout the centuries.

The iconographic scheme and the arrangement of frescoes within the church building initially achieved a certain rigidity: a three-zone hierarchical division from top to bottom. The lowest section of the walls was reserved for mortal personalities, the central part for the miraculous world of the Bible, and the upper section for the Kingdom of Heaven. The closed space around the altar was intended for the liturgical rites. The nave, accessible to the faithful, was painted with scenes from the gospels, while the porch, where the neophytes were confined, featured the horrors of the Last Judgement. Later fresco paintings started to show a Serbian local style and it was at that time that Serbia took over the lead from Byzantium.

Some of the earliest frescoes in existence today are those dating from the 12th century, which have partly survived in Djurdjevi Stupovi. These frescoes display all the characteristic features and styles used at the court of the Komnenos dynasty.

The fresco from Studenica, Mileševa (1225), the Church of Holy Apostles at Peć (1250), Morača (1260), Sopoćani (1264) and Arilje (1296) show a unique style based on classical proportions and classical ideals of beauty and they are almost perfect.

These paintings laid the foundations for 13th century Serbian art, the originals of which would eventually leave Serbia. They are the finest examples of the dynamic development, not only of Byzantine, but of European art in general.

Studenica frescoes

The princely monk and future archbishop, Sava Nemanjić, brought master painters with different artistic views from Constantinople in 1209 to paint Studenica; ten years later they went on to paint at Žiča.

The frescoes of Studenica are representative of the plastic style that became the main occupation of the 13th century painters. The artists of the frescoes at Studenica came over as very attractive in style; for the polishing Komnenos style they substituted their own compositions and are characterised, above all, by their monumental proportions, solemn and noble silence in the expression of feelings.

The frescoes at Studenica are of great dimensions; the figures are full of movement; the drawing is confidently and broadly handled and there is a rich sense and range of colours. Almost the entire wall space of this chapel is covered with portraits of historical figures and biographical compositions glorifying the Nemanjić family.

right: Crucifixion - Studenica monastery (detail)
In the face of Christ is depicted, and successfully emphasised, his divine nature and victory over death.

overleaf: Crucifixion - Studenica monastery

60

Crucifixion - Studenica monastery (details)

above: In the face of Virgin Mary the artist emphasised that adoration of God is stronger than material grief.

far left: On the other hand, John's grief is conveyed by gesture, not by facial expression. In this way the painter emphasised that faith is more important than human sorrow.

left: Beautifully painted, the dress of the Roman soldier Longinus, who suddenly realised his error while carrying out the punishment.

Žiča – Church of the Ascension

Žiča was founded jointly by Stefan "the First Crowned" and his son, King Radoslav. St Sava chose Žiča as the main seat of the Serbian church. In this church the coronation of the first Serbian king, Stefan, was performed.

The architectural style of the church, dedicated to the Ascension, represents the mature Raška school. It is a single nave structure with a massive cupola. On the east side is a broad, semicircular apse and it has closed vestibules on the north and south sides. On the western side is a narthex with a small lateral chapel. The fresco paintings date from two periods; the first period around the time of St Sava and they bear a close resemblance to the painting of Studenica monastery. Notable among them is the Crucifixion and the others are outstanding paintings of the early 14th century. These were painted during the reign of King Milutin and they are considered to be some of the finest Byzantine paintings of the first quarter of the 14th century.

Arilje

left: The present church was built by King Dragutin in 1296. It belongs to the 13th century Raška style, influenced by both Romanesque and Gothic styles. The church is monumental single-naved with a dome; the ground plan is that of a regular Greek cross.

The fresco painting in the church is ranked among the finest achievements of medieval Serbian art.

below:The impressive portraits of King Dragutin (holding the model of the church), his wife Katalina and his brother King Milutin, are considered masterpieces of 13th century portrait painting.

Mileševa

The monastery at Mileševa was founded by King Vladislav. After Studenica, Mileševa is, in terms of privileges and influence, the next most important monastery, its privileged position due partly to St Sava, the first archbishop, who was buried there.

The Bosnian King Tvrtko's coronation was held in this monastery.

The Mileševa church is an exceptional example of the Raška school. The church has a single nave surmounted by a dome, a large altar apse and side chapels. The Mileševa frescoes rank among the finest in European painting of the early 13th century.

The most remarkable in terms of composition and treatment of colours are: The Angel at Christ's tomb (White Angel), The Deposition, The Annunciation, Judas's Betrayal and Christ's Prayer in the Garden of Gethsemane. The portraits of the early Nemanjićs that have been preserved at Mileševa are deeply significant in Serbian cultural history. Portraits of St Sava, Stefan "the First Crowned" and his sons, Radoslav and Vladislav, were painted with an exquisite gift for realistic observation, especially the model traits of character and personality. They were painted during their lifetime and have been preserved for posterity. King Vladislav was painted with a model of his endowment.

Mileševa frescoes

The first decades of 13th century art in Serbia are truly a miracle. The indigenous painters, after receiving a few lessons from Greek artists, themselves became interpreters and masters of a newly awakened classical art, and by 1260 the Serbian artisans found themselves masters of classical forms. The best example of the summit of this art were paintings in the churches and monasteries of Mileševa and Sopćani.

The artists of King Vladislav painted their frescoes with a special technique. The whole mortar background was first dyed with a lively ochre and then subsequently covered with thin sheets of gold. In this way old-fashioned themes of paintings from antiquity were restored to a new life and transfigured by direct likeness between the old painting and the living beauty around them. The Mileševa artists managed skilfully to depict fine details of classical beauty of faces, proportion and skill of composition and above all by its tremendous scope and power.

They infused the paintings with such unrepeatable freshness, with such irradiating light and brilliance and with such personal enthusiasm, that their creativity presented the spectator with revelation, joy, experience and mystery.

Therefore, the Mileševa painting is striking for its modesty and essential human beauty which is occasionally inspired by the paintings of monumental character, but more often by models to be found in the paintings of miniatures.

Nowhere else are there to be found so many young and beautiful faces, so much noble beauty and strength in older people, nor more impressive and grandiose dimensions.

left: The paintings of Mileševa are intimate and of great beauty. The most beautiful of all is the biblical virtuoso fresco of the Angel at Christ's Tomb, popularly called "The White Angel". This painting is considered outstanding for its wonderful colours and nobility of countenance and gesture. It represents a version of the biblical story of the encounter between the angel and two women visiting Christ's tomb.

Mileševa

above left: St Macarius

above right: Moses the Prophet

top right: The Assumption I (details)

bottom right: The Final Judgment (detail)
—The Prophet

Mileševa

left: Jonah

right: Simeon Nemanja

During the middle of the 13th century political circumstances and the material wealth of Serbia, the product of its natural resources, particularly in mining and a thriving trade with coastal towns notably Dubrovnik and Venice, and the intellectual atmosphere and artistic tastes of the Serbian court of King Uroš I, all lent themselves to the development of art in this region of the Balkans.

There was a long period of peace and prosperity, that was a period of progress for this soundly organised state. The cultural climate was conducive to the production of translations into Serbian language of great ecclesiastical works and writings of the ancient philosophers, as well as the works of native writers commissioned by the King Uroš himself and his nobles.

69

Sopoćani

Sopoćani monastery was founded through an endowment from King Uroš I along with the church of the Holy Trinity, 1260.

This is one of the most beautiful churches in Serbia. It was intended as a royal mausoleum and to guard the tombs of the King's mother, Anna Dondolo, grand-daughter of the Venetian doge and the King's close family.

The principal intention of King Uroš I in building this church was to atone for his own sins, and the saint to whom the church was dedicated became the founder's intermediary with Christ at the Last Judgement.

At the time the monastery and churches were powerful religious and cultural centres and were invariably intended to become mausoleums for their founders and their families.

top right: The Monastery of Sopoćani

bottom right: The Church of the Holy Trinity, Sopoćani

The church is a triple-nave Romanesque basilica surmounted by a large dome with a tall bell-tower (built during the reign of Emperor Dušan).

Characteristic of the church is its architectural simplicity and the harmony of its design. The calm horizontal lines are characteristics of the Morava school.

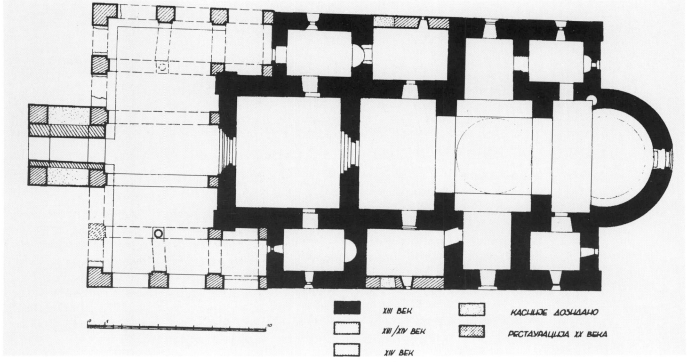

	XIII ВЕК		КАСНИЈЕ ДОЗИДАНО
	XIII/XIV ВЕК		РЕСТАУРАЦИЈА XX ВЕКА
	XIV ВЕК		

Sopoćani Frescoes

The culmination of the Raška school of painting lay in the frescoes of Sopoćani. These differ greatly from the paintings at Mileševa. The qualities which raise them to the highest artistic level are their exceptional balance of design, colour, plastic forms and sense of proportion, together with a fantastic sense of monumental figure-work. These great scenes are powerful, well designed and dramatic. In their paintings reality and imagination are drawn logically and with certain characteristics which can be found in classical paintings.

The complicated problems of monumental composition, masterful drawing, exquisite light and the intensity of the parts exposed to the light make the painted figures look strong and robust. This style of painting was unknown to the Byzantine world, either before or after, but this new concept and style of painting became closer to reality and represented the summit and the end of genuine monumental painting in medieval Serbia. Sopoćani masters were among the greatest European 13th century painters, creating a style which could not be repeated.

left: Apostle Paul

right: Apostle Peter

Sopoćani
above and right:
The Assumption of the Virgin (details)

Sopoćani: *The Assumption of the Virgin (details)*

*far left: The central figures are surrounded by disciples
and faithful. The grief was depicted in their gestures
and bowed heads.*

*left: Christ giving the soul of His mother to an angel.
In Byzantine art, the soul is often depicted as a tiny
human figure.*

Sopoćani

above left: The Virgin

above: John the Apostle

left: Vault of St Simeon (Nemanja)

right: The Adoration of the Martyrdom (details)

80

Sopoćani

top left and middle: Scroll of Solomon the Prophet (details)

top right and above right: Final Judgement (detail)

above left: The Descent into Hades (detail)

right: St Mark the Evangelist

Sopoćani

above left: The Unbelieving Thomas

above right: Nativity (detail)

right: King Stefan "The First Crowned" and King Uroš I

Gradac Monastery

The monastery at Gradac was founded by Queen Jelena of Anjou, wife of King Uroš I. She ordered the construction of the foundations when her elder son, Stefan Dragutin was crowned.

It is also believed that the queen maintained a convent school there, where young ladies of noble families could acquire a general education. Queen Jelena was buried in Gradec in 1314.

The architecture of the monastery is typical of the Raška school, with a strong influence of gothic. Among the existing frescoes is a fragment of an historic composition which probably depicts the death of King Uroš I. This is the closest existing example of the splendid work of the Sopoćani painters.

Gradac Monastery

above: The Annunciation

left: The Nativity

Patriarchate of Peć

The complex buildings known as Patriarchate of Peć date from the 13th and 14th centuries. From the 13th century until 1776, Peć was the seat of the Serbian Orthodox Church. Initially a Serbian archbishopric and in 1346, the Patriarchate. The oldest church is the Holy Apostles, a typical example of the Raška architectural style. There is a possibility that there was an even older building which was remodelled in the 13th century after the Church of Žiča, with the addition of the dome - the composition of the Ascension. Christ, larger than life in shimmering robes of gold, dominates the whole church. The virgin is portrayed in an earlier style.

During the 14th century two single-nave churches were built onto the Holy Apostles: The Church of St Demetrius to the north and the Church of St Mary to the South.

The frescoes in both churches are 14th century, executed in the narrative style of the Palaelogian Revival. The name of the artist was Jovan, who, with a group of painters, decorated Garčanica and several other churches, which, iconographically, show work of unequal quality.

The Church of St Demitrius and the Church of St Mary

The dome of St Demitrius rests on pilasters, whereas the dome of St Mary is supported by free-standing columns. Another small church, dedicated to St Nicholas, was built on to the south wall of St Mary's. The narthex originally opened like a portico and was considered a masterpiece of construction. These 14th century buildings were made of bricks and stone in alternating layers, a decorative device enlivening the exterior, which owes a lot to Byzantine building techniques.

If no account is taken of the historical and chronological order of the period during which these monuments were built, but style alone were the only consideration as the basic criterion, then we should include in this group the churches of Banjska, Dečani and St Archangels, built a little later in the 14th century.

The Holy Apostles in Peć

This belongs to the Peć Patriarch complex of churches, once the seat of the Serbian archbishops and patriarchs. The plan is typical of the Raška School in having a single aisle, transept, dome and a broad space for the altar which ends in a large apse and two side apses.

The oldest frescoes date from the mid 13th century and occupy the dome, the space beneath it, and the altar. Original frescoes have been preserved in the sanctuary, the cupola and the upper parts of the area under the cupola. The painters of the portraits, which are of variable quality, are now known, but they succeeded in painting one of the most beautiful Serbian frescoes of the late 13th century, in the oldest, preserved cycle of the Passion of Christ.

The richly worked composition, with many participants whose distribution in space is considerably freer, is subordinated to the real relationship between the figures, the architecture and the landscape.

The Ascension of Christ (details):

*left: Outstanding among the other paintings is the
large Ascension of Christ in the cupola. A grandiose
composition in which Christ, shining in robes of gold,
dominates by virtue of being larger than life.*

*above: Ascension, Angel
In the Holy Apostles the portraits are idealised;
stern and grave with emaciated features.*

right: Ascension, Paul

far right: Ascension, Apostles

Holy Apostles, Peć

above left and right:
Ascension, Apostles

right: John the Evangelist

far right: Deises,
Madonna

Holy Apostles, Peć

above: Assumption Madonna
High in the church dome of the church is the monumental
figure of the mother of God, Ornata, painted around
1260 with the composition of the Assumption. The artist
followed strict stylistic rules. The Mother of God glows
with exceptional earthy beauty and is full of innocence and
grace. She is depicted with arms spread, the symbol of the
earthly church founded by her son.

left: The Holy Virgin Nursing Her Child
This fresco is an entirely independent creation by the
artist, who was inspired by the hymn to the Holy Virgin
written by the Constantinople Patriarch, Sergios.
   The Virgin is portrayed sitting on the throne nursing
her child, two angels are by her side in an attitude of
adoration, dressed in imperial costumes; above and on the
side are a group of girls saluting the Virgin. The painter
has made a simple composition which is unusually fine
and spiritual.

Holy Apostles, Peć

left: Madonna
The Virgin is characterised by gentle contours, express-
ly tonal values and the relationship between light and
shade; which represents a reaction against the bright,
luxuriant colouring of the Sopoćani Monastery School.

above: Madonna's Birth (detail)

The Western Arcade, Peć

far left: Deisis (detail)
In the altar apse is depicted the Deisis, a monumental
painting of the figure of Christ on the throne; with
St John and the Mother of God turning to Him in a
prayer for mankind.

above: Pilot Washes His Hands (detail)

left: The Washing of the Feet (detail)

99

left/right: Christ's Martyrdom (detail)

Western Arcade, Peć

above: Christ's Martyrdom (detail)

left: Nativity (detail)

right: The Holy Communion (detail)

far left: Judas's Betrayal, Peć

Western Arcade, Peć

left: The Bishop's Mass (detail)

above left: Archangel Gabriel
In the Christian religion, archangels represent a specific
kind of angel. They are the spiritual beings of the
'Upper World' that surround God, and carry out his
ideas on earth. Here Archangel Gabriel is depicted as a
man of God.

above right: Archbishop Danilov II

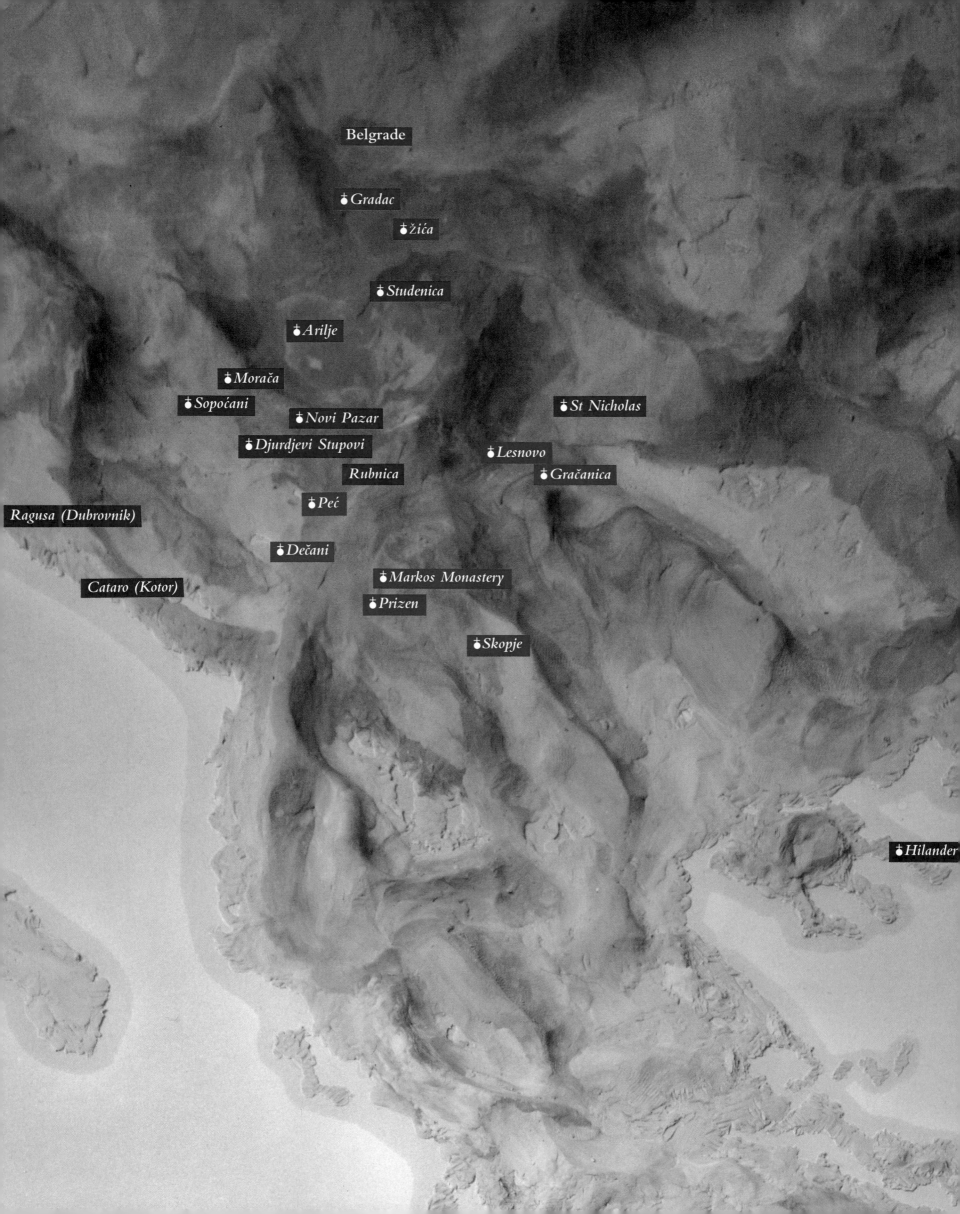

Belgrade

⚜ *Gradac*

⚜ *Žiča*

⚜ *Studenica*

⚜ *Arilje*

⚜ *Morača*

⚜ *Sopoćani*

⚜ *St Nicholas*

⚜ *Novi Pazar*

⚜ *Djurdjevi Stupovi*

⚜ *Lesnovo*

Rubnica

⚜ *Gračanica*

⚜ *Peć*

Ragusa (Dubrovnik)

⚜ *Dečani*

⚜ *Markos Monastery*

Cataro (Kotor)

⚜ *Prizen*

⚜ *Skopje*

⚜ *Hilander*

Chapter Three

KING MILUTIN'S SCHOOL

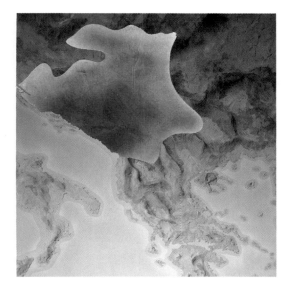

Map of Serbia under King Milutin

An important turning-point in the development of the territories of Serbia was the introduction of mining, which was introduced into Serbia at the end of the 13th century and the beginning of the 14th. The Serb rulers imposed taxes on the mines, which brought them large revenues. The merchants made considerable profits from the exporting of silver, electrum and gold, and the peasant population also enjoyed the benefits because they supplied all the mining communities with what they required in the way of food, milk etc. The permanent presence of coastal merchants resulted in good communication with manufacturing centres of other countries and a comparatively good supply of fabrics and manufactured goods which were in demand. In any event, Serbia was, at the end of the Middle Ages, a highly developed and certainly not a backward country.

The richest ruler in the Balkans during that time was the Serbian King Milutin (Stefan Uroš II) who managed to take over the considerable riches flowing from the country's seven large silver and gold mines. He introduced a tremendous wave of Byzantine influences to all areas of life, including politics and the arts.

The luxury of King Milutin's court was far greater than that of the Byzantine equivalent. The Minister of Emperor Andronicus, Theodore Metochite, recorded that Milutin himself was sumptuously dressed; his court glittered with silk, gold and precious stones and visitors to his court were served all kinds of food on plates of gold and silver; in fact everything Metochite said was in accordance with Roman (ie Byzantine) taste and the ceremonial trappings of the Imperial court.

Another way in which King Milutin's court emulated that of the Byzantine's was in the introduction of their terminology into official documents, and in the introduction of numerous and complicated Byzantine honourific titles into the Serbian court.

He was ambitious and energetic, but pious in a rather flamboyant way, and he established and decorated numerous monasteries and churches. It was the wealth that derived from the mines that made it possible for him to carry out his lavish building programme.

Archbishop Danilo said that the king built all these endowments with thoughts of the Last Judgement. He believed that Christ would have no mercy on those who did not give alms, though it is arguable that the king may have done these good deeds for political reasons. By building mainly bishoprics, he wanted to ensure that he had the churches' powerful organisation backing him and his policies.

Architecture

On the other hand, King Milutin may have made these endowments from his personal inclination and love of the beauty of art, wishing to glorify his own memory. The king may have erroneously thought that works of art brought the founder immortality.

At the end of the 13th century, the development of Serbian art began to stagnate and the great achievements of Mileševa and Sopoćani began to disappear. The new revival symbolically coincided with the great conquest of King Milutin in the southern regions of Macedonia. Political changes in the 14th century, besides bringing with them territorial and economic modifications, also brought about changes in the manner of constructing and decorating churches and monasteries in medieval Serbia.

A new style based on the artistic conceptions of the Constantinople Palaeologue Revival, is present in all the churches built under the auspices of and during the reign of King Milutin. This style reached Serbia via Macedonia at the beginning of the 14th century and it became established as the official court style of that period called Milutin's Era. Although the exact date of the beginning of Milutin's Era is hard to establish, it is generally considered that the first church of the list of monuments he founded was the main church at Hilandar.

In reality, this type of building was only new to the Serbs. It was originally based on an old Oriental and Byzantine model called the Inscribed Cross, similar types of which can be found in all regions dominated by the Byzantine influence, although it had never been used or appreciated before by the Serbs. Hence no trace of Roman influence or style can be found in the churches built during Milutin's Era, in essence they are all Byzantine in style.

All new churches adopted the Byzantine architectural pattern; their ground plan was in the form of an inscribed cross, with between one and five domes. Their facades were built of alternative courses of stone and brick and they were enlivened by polychromatic brickwork in the form of a chessboard design, meandering, zigzagging and crossing to and fro. What was lost in interior space was sometimes compensated for by the lively rhythm of their external volume.

The main monuments of this group are the territory of today's Kosovo and the best examples still surviving are St Bogorodica Ljeviška at Gračanica Prizren, the King's Church at Studenica, Peć and many others in modern-day Macedonia.

Gračanica Monastery

It was always recognised that Gračanica was one of the most outstanding monasteries in a group of six surviving churches built by King Milutin. Construction started circa 1313. The style was highly innovative, the architectural design evolving from what is by now known as the Byzantine-Serbian school, which stressed monumental expressiveness.

Gračanica is distinguished by its vertical and pyramid composition, with a balance and symmetry unequalled in many other Byzantine five-domed churches. Gračanica differed from all other contemporary churches built in Constantinople, Salonika and Serbia itself, by the richness of imagination and the beauty of its concept.

Gračanica is taller than any previously built Serbian church. The cupola rises to a height of twenty metres, borne upon four very slim columns each ten metres high. They support two crosses, superimposed one upon the other, on which the cupola rests.

The most interesting effect of this architecture is displayed outside, where the pyramid shape of the building is gained through a graduated mass, to which the small cupolas were placed lower than the main one. The arches beneath each cupola break in order, to emphasise the highest point, visually. The main cupola crowns this masterpiece of medieval architecture.

Gračanica Monastery – *elevations*

Windows of the Studencia Monastery

left: These are the most richly ornamental, especially the three-light window of the alter apse. They are beautifully decorated with copious sculptures in the Roman style which are chiselled in the marble, and were typical of the Raška School. The copy of the three-light window from the Studencia Monastery was applied in the Dečani Monastery nearly 150 years later.

Windows of the Gračania Monastery

left: Ornamentation of the edifices during King Milutin's reign are in stone, alternating with brick-work. A single trace of Roman style can be found on all these churches, but only the Byzantine decoration of the windows of Gracanica is typical — using the forms of zigzaging and crossing to and fro.

above and opposite page: Gospel of the Serbian Metropolitan Bishop Jacob (British Library)

Literature

During the 13th and 14th centuries literature in Serbia received a strong impetus. The protagonists of Serbian literature were members of the ruling dynasty and the most learned monks. Medieval Serbia became the focal point of extensive cultural and artistic work during this period of prosperity. Members of King Milutin's dynasty and the nobility enjoyed the closest relations with other courts of Europe. They cultivated elegant tastes as show in contemporary style. They founded libraries and provided monks with the raw material for their literary, artistic and scientific work.

The monasteries were the cradles of this literary activity. The monks were usually educated at Mount Athos, where they copied and translated books primarily for the requirements of their monasteries and other churches in Serbia. The literature included every known manuscript in Byzantine literature, starting with ritual books and finishing with philosophical, ethical and oratorical works. In addition, there were annals and chronicles, hagiographies and legends.

Besides their religious and historical value, the Serbian biographies also had special national significance. They steadily raised the consciousness of Serbia, its mission, and the aggrandisement of the Serbian state and the difficulties its rulers encountered.

Until the 14th century Serbian books and scrolls were written on parchment in monasteries and at court; the use of paper did not begin until later in the 14th century. Text was written in black or brown ink, titles and initials in red or sometimes blue. Stately and solemn luxury books, titles and initials, as well as those parts of the text which needed to be emphasised, were all written in gold. The same masters wrote, designed and painted manuscripts, prepared ink and paints and bound books. Some of the masters even painted frescoes in churches. They were the most literate personages among the artists. The most well known Serbian name of this time was Theodore Gramatic, who has left behind lengthy records and inscriptions about himself and his life on Mount Athos, where he wrote several books for King Uroš. Serbian miniatures were produced during the reigns of King Milutin and Tsar Dušan. Some of the manuscripts of that time match the best works of Constantinople. About the mid-14th century Serbian transcribers made luxurious manuscripts such as Nikola Stanjevic's gospel and the gospel of Serbian Metropolitan Bishop Jakob (now held in the British Library), whose transcriber was Kalis.

The lives of King Uroš, King Dragutin, Queen Jelena, King Milutin, Stefan Dečanski and King Dušan were written at that time by Danilo of Peć and his pupil Georgije. Parts of Danilo's biographies of the lives of the Serbian kings and archbishops, which were written in the 14th century, are distinguished by great realistic descriptions, and clear pictures of the conditions that prevailed in the Balkans at that time. He wrote about travellers and attacks by highwaymen on the roads of Serbia. All these biographies have special national significance. They often describe vividly the lifestyle of the Serbian people, the relations which prevailed among the Serbian nobility, the position of the church and the way of life of ordinary Serbs.

Although church books (the Quardi Gospels and Psalters, the lives of saints, etc.) still dominated, remarkable secular works flourished, like tales and romances about Alexander the Great, the Trojan War and the Empress Theophani. The most important written work of the 14th century is the Emperor Dušan's famous and detailed law-code, known as the Zakonik, which he first promulgated in 1349: just before his death he issued an expanded version. Dušan's Zakonik, which provides so many fascinating pictures of the social and economic condition of Serbs in the mid 14th century, is one of the great documents of medieval Europe and deserves to be better known.

Ѿ МАТѲЕА, СТОЕВАГ҃ЛІО

в[ъ]ствованиѥ, глава, прьва

К҃нигародьства Іу҃ Хв҃а, сн҃а дв҃а

сн҃а авраамлга ⁘ авраамь

роди ісаака · ісаакже ро

ди іакова · іаковже

роди іоудоу · и братию его ·

іоуда же роди фареса · и

зара ѿ ѳамары · фарес же роди

пе, прехо х҃вѣль ст҃ыхъ ѡц҃ь

dot · te oŝo cruno chaie uzachonu prauadnich da ono
cruno chaie usuero uangeliu od pridobrich · sic cu
sea prauadna guie ubozim · i odiua nagoeha i gliubi
ilearenega suoga oteha lenu huderi neciny riç mora
uadnu · i laz neouorit · te rici usaarzele · u starom za
chonu · da suak lenie oistine suetoga uangelia ouacho
zapouida · Ne pʃły opeta dueh tuoy od onega chi uagel
tebi gnega iest · i da day blaga tuoga onim chi od tr
be pʃetga · sac nesamo osalochienie podnesty gima
se · o a yʃuangosche stuariy ioschie sradostiu podnesty
gimaiutse · ij tolichoie ioschie · u brime potribgliuo
ziuot sa brata suoga podlozity gimase · O uacha dusea
milosardna iest · a ne ona cha samo ustuar suirou
nu smilouaie naisearenega ima · E ffacha cha uidi alit
slisaty bude nichu stuar cha giseargnich oʒaloschiuie
i gimity bude smilouaie nagnicf · u saŗŋ suoie · u gi
stinu ta tacha dusa milosardna yest · ij tolichoie ona
milosardna iest cha chada od sestre biena budet suoie
nerecet stuari niedne chabi oʒalostila sarçe gneie ;

OdBdinia Lapitul orughy ·· 3 ····

Jmiete piecinno delouanie od Bdinya saç da
naydete · u tiseenie chochiese yblizaty eduseam
uaseim · M · Astoy · u Ztéiu sama · saç pamer tua da

С̑де́снꙋ̈ю ст҃а́го хлѣ́ба
бли́зь среды̀, е̑го́ гл҃е.
Пре̑дьста цр҃ица ѡ̑десꙋ̈ю,
тебѣ̀, в̈ри́зꙋ̈ позлаще́-
ны̀ ѡ̑де́тапа пре̑хꙋ́крашенна:
та́же, пріе́мь тре́тїю.
Про̑форꙋ́. гл҃е: С̑и́лою
ӵт҃нⷮаго н҃животво̑ре́щаго
кⷬта. ꙋ̈́ны нь́ны сил̈ьбе-
зпль́ны ꙋ̈ньна́го н̃сла́внаго

dusca poçmosi Tribulationi· i telschochie· suesclie· tada
more· sauudaz hratreno zala misglienia saçbo misglicia
poçubgliuiurse telschochiom· E hada dusca spominase·
odsuuich· orihouf· i muçi sama sebe· tada bog· oimaidhie
pomoru da ucini onu· u lacheinj poçimuij· saç bg uese
litse dasy sama sebi dusca daio muchu· cichia prua
rema puta suoga· cha stuar iest zlamenie· od pochore·
y cholicho choly ui daiere uechiu muchu same seby· i
dusci uascoj tolicho uechie bog uzmnozuie plachiu·
uascu· F sacha radost ch usroch ni· od criposty· tudie
usciuise ganutie od pozelinia u onoj cha nahodit rado
st onu ps usrucha cripostiy a to razumjeti· od flachog
pozelinia zlobnoga da ne Norantchoga

          od vaslicich napastij· i chachoie· u gnich
          starchost chase cini cripostiu· i od scha
          lim· i od redij pochich dusca razumma·
          hodi nasem suitu· Capi· trideset· i osam· —

Edna cripost ushodi na druchu· saç da ni·
iedna ni druga nebude telscha ni trudna· i sa
da se criposty budu snaredbo uciçnene· i pota
put uedle laghglie criposti iesut· i sa da tacho·
naredno budu prichlone nadellouanie· a one·
zlobne dabudu nadobro prichlone· i dobre· tolichoie·

                                                          hiiii·

Od naucha chordna i ostay   ja Rač   boze...

Siut zeoufni ... dar ... qu dobna nir a
obluqiena sac u ... ... iest zlamenie pameti zlo
bom rac mazane i poriceth nag ... elsaquele ... smuter
gne che u dusei iessu R. e doufnica nep ... ...
uoreie suitofno R. e doufnica budi uazda sudij suogimi baechi
i ne ochagliarse staschimim misgliciem Glubi mudrost pisma
suetoga a ne gliubi mudrost tellesnu R. e doufnica cha gliubg
liechi zeli ysucast niedne ostale stuari nedofegise uiditi da is
chupglia fruty pbiuauchi u razui od rasluçita pism boza tue
ga Suotsu naslagieia gueie i souima ogagliuie duscu suoiu
R. e doufnica gurig simplicitas colubice iedne nij misli zlo od
sestre ni guscagne suoie Ziuot razune dusce iest misliti od
smaty Onda redofnica suditse chada ona cinitse naymagu od assich
L ... por redofnice iest biti blidi y humiglieni sa obrazo mledni
Asho ti budes mochy mucaty i podnesti oslaglaseie i obreceie i ne
ueglie i pogargeie to iest cripost puelidia i lety suahu zapouidij
ostalich R. e doufnica cha prossy nazemgli giminia ona niti zedo
ufnica e Tha cholye zbogom ona razuna i blacena iest Blazen
 y iedignieie suetoschy i poznania criposty iest i cinitse po
Delouaniu dobrom ... ... a, m, e, n, :-

DEO GRACIAS

XV. KL. NOB

FINIS

H

·1514·

In Dušan's Code, approved by the Assembly in 1349, the Emperor promised protection to church property and exempted church states from taxation. The church had little say in political decisions of the time, except within the framework of the Assembly. Therefore the church appeared as an equal partner with the nobility when representing the people.

Alexander the Great, whose life is probably considered to be one of the best known of the romantic biographies of the time, was particularly popular with the Serbs, so much so that Russian scribes who copied it from the original Serbian manuscripts called it the Serbian Alexandrid. The saga of Alexander the Great was evidently regarded not only as light literature but also as a practical guide to popular traditional literature.

below: The Hilandar transcript is deposited today in the Hilandar Monastery, Mount Athos.

Paintings

The monumental style of the 13th century began to stagnate. The great achievements of Mileševa and Sopoćani vanished and the frescoes of the 14th century evolved under the influence of the new style of painting began with deeper spaces, little figures in lovely movements, larger landscape in the background and decorative buildings of fantastic architecture. This new style was formed at Constantinople, known at that time as the Palaeologue Revival or Renaissance.

The church paintings included a great number of new highly complicated iconographical themes which tried to give as much information as possible through the pictures, which were designed in such a way as to educate the illiterates via their painted subjects and written text of the events Portrayed. This was the beginning of the Narrative Style.

Skilful drawing and the intensive colouring of refined gamut, which sometimes turns into mannerism, are the characteristics of these paintings. As the size of the paintings decreased the number of figures increased. Paintings of the King Milutin era are far richer in the detail of everyday life. The artists were more absorbed by the themes than by the spiritual and theological experience.

King Milutin himself engaged a group of artists, well-known names of the time such as Astrapa, Michael and Eutychious, to carry the decoration and ornamentation of his numerous foundations.

These great scenic paintings were presented in firm outlines, and contained powerful draughtsmanship and strongly contrasting colours, which suggested a unique power of expression and a trend toward plasticity, characteristic of these three artists. They were commissioned to paint King Milutin's pious foundations: the church of the city of Skopje, the church of the Virgin Ljeviš.

The king's church at Studenica has the most beautiful representation of Palaeologue paintings, a style which introduced some interesting features in its iconography, i.e. scenes of everyday life and its genre; the happy mother, the Virgin, lays her cheek lovingly on that of her child, Joseph is preoccupied with his doubts, the shepherds are eagerly listening to the angels singing. Everything is the result of discriminating taste with many beautiful details, lots of silk, embroidery, draperies and in shades of greyish blue, dark blue and greyish white, the glimmer of silk and velvet, the faces of beautiful young girls who look distinguished and noble, parts of landscape architecture are the new scenes in the painting of the early 14th century.

above: West side of the King's Church, Studenica.

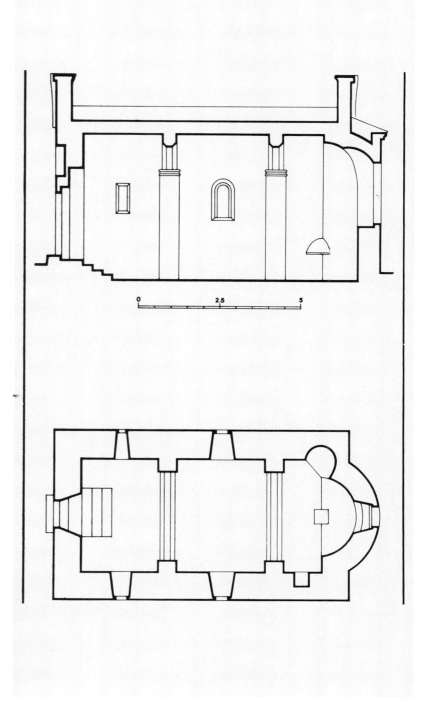

above: Ground-plan and cross-section. It was the work of an experienced master-builder. The ground plan belongs to the 'reduced inscribed cross-type'.

King's Church, Studenica

The Birth of the Virgin Mary
This important composition in the King's Church
shows scenes from the life of the Virgin Mary and her
parents.

above: The Bathing of the Infant (detail)

left: Birth of the Virgin Mary

King's Church, Studenica

above/right: The Birth of the Virgin Mary

King's Church, Studenica

Christ's Nativity, (1313-14)
*This painting of the Nativity, the most beautiful repre-
sentative of Palaeologue painting, has introduced some
new interesting features in its inconography: scenes of
everyday life: a happy mother, the Virgin, leaning her
cheek lovingly on that of the new-born baby; the angels
rejoicing; an angel announcing the birth to the shepherds, who are eagerly listening to the angel's voice; the
bathing of the infant Messiah and the arrival of the
Wise Men of the East, led by the star of Bethlehem
and an angel of the Lord.*

Birth of Christ (details)

*top: The fresco illustrating events from the history of
Christianity often depict episodes portraying the everyday life of man. Bathing the new-born Christ, with a
girl pouring warm water.*

*bottom: The shepherd - an old man and the youth,
depicted with a herd of sheep are shown in this detail
from the fresco.*

King's Church, Studenica

*The Presentation of the Virgin in the Temple (details),
In the King's Church there are many beautiful details:
lots of silk embroidery, draperies in shades of blue and
white. Stylistically, the frescoes belong to Byzantine
Palaeologue art of the early 14th century. The majestic
composition aspires to a classical beauty through a feel-
ing of serenity and restrained movements. The painting
is probably the work of the famous artists from
Salonika, Michael and Eutychios.*

King's Church, Studenica

*The Communion of Apostles: this composition of The
Communion of Apostles is halved: Christ officiating
twice, first proffering bread, (left) then wine (right).*

King's Church, Studenica

left: Communion of the Appostles (detail)

*right: The portrait of St Sava, depicting his long
energetic red face, greying beard and discerning eyes,
with unremitting creative energy and goodwill; the
face of one of the most unique inteilects of the
medieval era.*

In the place of honour in the passage between the narthex and nave are portraits of King Milutin, holding a model of the church, and Queen Simonida, his wife.

In this fresco, Christ is depicted above the King, blessing him and sending, through His angels, the crown - a symbol of the divine nature of his earthly power.

Opposite Milutin, in contrast, stands the portrait of his young wife, Simonida. Her tender face painted in the fashion of the 14th century, completely flat, without modelling still radiates a refined beauty.

left: King Milutin, Gračanica Monastery
Next to the King's portrait is written "Stefan Uroš faithful to Christ by divine grace autocratic king of all the Serbs by land and by sea and founder"

right: Queen Simonida, Gračanica Monastery
Next to Queen Simonida is written "Simonida Palaeologa, daughter of Emperor Andronicus Palaeologus"

141

Gračanica Monastery

above: St Roman

left: St John the Baptist

opposite page:
top left: St John Lestvic
top right: St Vincent,
bottom left: St Meletius
bottom right: St Mercurius

Gračanica Monastery

above: The Omnipotent

right: The Prophet

below: detail from one of the Charters of Gračanica, the text of which was inscribed in fresco technique on a wall of the church and included the following:

"EMPEROR OF EMPERORS AND LORD OF LORDS, LIVING AND INACCESSIBLE LIGHT WHICH COMMANDS THE HEAVEN AND REIGNS OVER THE EARTH AND GOVERNS THE MIGHTY, WHO RULES LIFE AND DEATH. WHO ASCENDED THE HILL OF TABOR, WISHING TO SHOW HIS DISCIPLES THE LIGHT OF HIS DIVINE GLORY. LET US OURSELVES, POORER THAN ALL IN SPIRIT, HEART AND MIND, ENDEAVOUR TO REACH THE HEIGHT OF DIVINE CONDUCT, IN ORDER TO SEE THE GLORY OF OUR GOD, WHO, OUT OF HIS GREAT MERCY, WISHED TO FORGIVE MANKIND, BENUMBED BY SIN, SO THAT THOSE WHO LOOK FOR GOD CAN FIND HIM"

Gračanica Monastery

The frescoes in Gračanica came at the end of a brilliant period of Byzantine and Serbian art, the so-called Renaissance of the Palaeologue. The basic characteristic of Gračanica paintings is that the surfaces of the walls, vaults, pillars and arches are covered with cycles and compositions with many tiny figures, the events from the gospels are systematised in cycles which depict, in a clockwise direction, scenes from Christ's preaching, miracles and parables, His passion and appearance after His death.

above/right: The Marriage at Cana
This fresco shows a large number of guests, freely placed at the table, some with their backs to the observer, the place of honour given to the bride and bridegroom, attired in the aristocratic robes of that time.

All those frescoes with complex theological ideas of the early 14th century stand out with their simple composition and emphasised symmetry and in Gračanica they are expressed in early understandable pictorial language.

146

left: Laying of Christ in Tomb

below: Assumption of Madonna

Gračanica Monastery

above: Paradise.
One of the most impressive compositions in colouring is
*The Kingdom of Heaven, whose gates are guarded by
an angel. St Peter, accompanying the blessed to heav-
en, is approaching the Virgin, who sits enthroned with
angels on both sides, while Abraham holds the justice
in his lap.*

right: Scenes from Calendar (details)

Gračanica Monastery

far left: Holy Women in the Flames (detail)

left: St Mercurius, one of the Holy Warriors, brilliantly ornamented, fully armed, with cape flying and mighty sword in hand.

Gračanica Monastery

left: Scenes from The Last Judgement (details)
The painters of Gračanica faithfully portrayed nature,
plant life, tame birds and wild beasts.

right: Angel with Crown (detail)

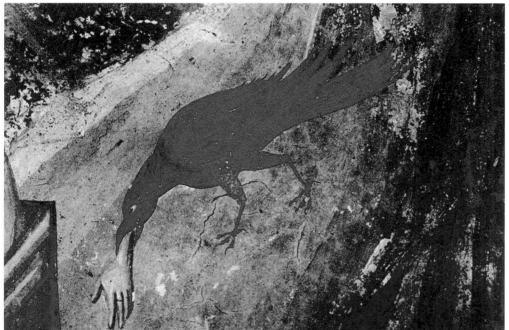

152

The second stage of Serbian medieval art is linked with the rule of King Milutin (1282 - 1321), a brave warrior, clever diplomat, and rich, refined patron of the arts. This period is called 'Milutin's Era'. King Milutin engaged a group of artists: Astrapa, Michael and Eutychious for the decoration of his numerous foundations. We know nothing of their schooling, but we do know that they were the main painters of Gračanica, Staro Nagoričano, Virgin of Ljeviš, King's Church at Studenica among others.

His son, Stefan Dečanski, ordered the monastery church at Dečani to be built. The painting of frescoes began in 1335, immediately after the construction of the church was completed. The paintings were completed during the reign of Emperor Dušan.

All the walls of the monastery were covered with numerous individual scenes: in all, over 1,000 compositions in lively colours, well preserved to this day.

The sorrows and vicissitudes of human existence are all to be found on the walls of Dečani: the crippled and the sick, the martyrs and the tormentors, the robbers and the sinners, peasants, men working in the fields and in the vineyards, fishermen, stonemasons and preachers are included in an unending procession.

About twenty mural compositions, with scenes from the Old and New Testaments, are illustrated with the whole church calendar and events from the lives of various saints. The most important portraits are found in the narthex, among them Stefan Dečanski, King Uroš, Emperor Dušan, his wife Jelena and their son Uroš. A very well preserved and important fresco is the Nemanjić family tree (see below).

The finest and most beautiful frescoes are to be seen in the cupola. A cycle with eleven scenes from the Great Festivals and the fresco of the Crucifixion. Two very interesting details are shown, the Sun and the Moon, which are similar to the space-ships of today, and certainly what looks like two human figures.

Paintings of High Dečani are the works of unknown masters from the Adriatic coast who were very well acquainted with Byzantine and Serbian artistic traditions. One of them has actually added his signature, "Srdj, the sinner" on the capital of the column near the very beautiful composition, The Creation of the World.

The Nemanjić Family Tree, Dečani

Dečani Monastery

Dečani is one of the most outstanding of Serbian medieval monasteries. The church was built between 1327 and 1335 and the founder was King Stefan Uroš III. Dečani is a large-domed, five-aisled type of basilica with a triple-naved narthex. The builder was Fra Vita of Kotor and the stonemasons also came from the coastal regions of the Adriatic.

The church has two additional altars (the north one, dedicated to St Demitrius, and the south dedicated to St Nicholas), a feature that does not occur in any of the orthodox churches of Serbia.

Sculptural ornamentation in the monastery of Dečani was, as already mentioned, carried out by Fra Vita's workshop; portals, windows and consoles were all made of marble. The altar window was a copy of the one at Studenica. The style of this building portrays Byzantine and Romanesque Gothic influences.

Dečani Monastery

below: Eastern triforium, tympanum drawing

right: Eastern triforium, general view

bottom left: Console of the pilaster, to the south of the eastern triforium

bottom right: Triforium (detail)

Dečani Monastery

top left: Northern portal, general view

right: Apostle Philip and Soaring Eagles

left: The Cherub in the Midst of the Vine Which Feeds the Pious-in-Christ

Dečani Monastery

top : *The Desert-Seeking Turtledove,*

middle : *The Meeting of Peace*

bottom : *Asp's Offspring*

158

Dečani Monastery

top : The Herb of Curacy

middle/bottom : Baptism of Christ

Dečani Monastery

top: Western facade (detail)

top right: Western facade

bottom right: St George slaying the Dragon and Saving the Princess

Dečani Monastery

top left: Griffin, inner portal

bottom left: Lion, the Enemy of Man, inner portal

161

Paintings

Although the paintings in High Dečani belong to the narrative style which is characteristic of the Palaeologue Renaissance, there are traces of individual frescoes of the monumental style of the 13th century, even hints of Morava paintings can be discerned.

Dečani is one of the few monasteries which have withstood the misfortunes and plunderings of five centuries. Its medieval treasures include richly illuminated manuscripts of the 13th century, costly vestments, precious church vessels and, above all, the celebrated icons of the Dečani School.

Dečani *The Western Wall*
Painting of the fresco began immediately after 1335 when construction of the church was finished; the paintings were finished during the reign of Emperor Dušan. All the walls were covered in frescoes, with over 1,000 compositions and about 10,000 figures.

The paintings are well preserved and the choice of them is well thought out.

Dečani Monastery

above: Christ with Apostles, fresco (detail)

left: The Acatist of Madonna, fresco (detail)

Dečani Monastery

above: Apostle Philip

left: Wedding in Cana, fresco (detail)

ГАЛАПТШОЇВЫПСГПС
ТНМЇ ѸСЕКНОВЕНА
БЫСТА

Dečani Monastery

left: Apostle Philip, fresco

right: Calendar (detail)

167

Dečani Monastery
Scenes from Calendar

Dečani Monastery

above: Christ Healing the Innocent (details)

opposite: Christ Healing the Rabid (detail)

172

Dečani Monastery

above/opposite: Scenes from The Last Judgment, frescoes

Dečani Monastery
Christ's Miracles, fresco (details)

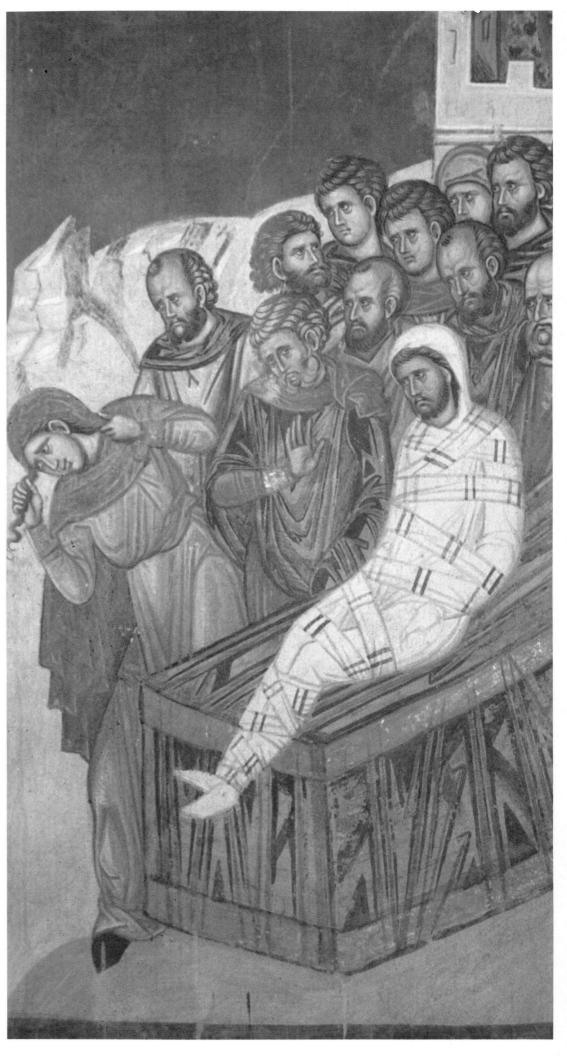

Hilandar, Mount Athos

A monastery has existed at Hilandar since the 10th century, but it had already been abandoned when Stefan Nemanja, founder of the Serbian dynasty, renounced his throne to become the monk Simeon.

The present monastery has buildings of various periods, including two towers remaining largely intact from Simeon and Sava's foundations. Its form is essentially as reconstructed and enlarged by King Milutin in 1293, when he rebuilt the main church and the refectory.

The monasteries of Mount Athos were generally free from interference during the period of Turkish occupation of the Balkans, and were able to retain their links with all orthodox countries and preserve their rich heritage of gifts offered by royal patrons through the Middle Ages. The icons alone number in the hundreds, the earliest coming from the 12th century, the mosaic icon of Hilandar, which originally occupied the prime place of honour in Simeon and Sava's church.

In the monastery there are also about 330 Greek and Serbian charters, manuscripts and early printed books.

The Monastery of Hilandar

The Mount Athos, Holy Mountain, is situated at the most easterly of the three fingers of Chalcidice (Greece). The monks call it "the garden of the most Holy Mother of God" which came from the legend that after Christ's ascension, the Virgin Mother set out for Cyprus to visit the resurrected Lazarus, but a miraculous storm carried her ship to Athos. Here she recieved divine instruction to preach the gospel: "This place shall be your salvation for those who desire to be saved".

On Mount Athos is one of the most beautiful monasteries, Hilandar, whose founders were Stefan Nemanja, the Grand Župan and his youngest son St Sava.

The Byzantine Emperor, Alexious, gave permission for them to rebuild the monastery as "a gift in perpetuity to the Serbs" as stated in his edict of 1198. Stefan Nemanja's son Stefan, "The First Crowned", provided the financial support for its construction on the site of the ruins of an old Greek monastery.

During the Middle Ages, the Serbian rulers (King Milutin, King Dečanski, Tsar Dušan, Prince Lazar being especially generous) continued to support the monastery, and it became from the beginning the most important religious, cultural and national centre of the Serbs, making a great contribution to the development of literacy, literature and art in general.

At the same time Hilandar was a spiritual link with the Byzantine world and had a great influence in all the regions of Serbia and areas where Serbians lived.

The Hilandar monastery preserved a large collection of ancient icons, utensils, corporals, vestments, embroideries etc. along with a huge number of manuscripts, including imperial and ecclesiastic edicts (280 written in Greek and 150 in Serbian Old Church Slavonic).

The monastery gave to Serbia patriarchs, archbishops and many bishops and attracted a large number of monks and learned people from Serbia throughout its past and right up to modern times.

Hilandar, Mount Athos

Icon of Theotokos Hodegeria (c. 1200),
This is the patron icon of Hilandar Monastery, and it
is believed that the Grand Župan, Stefan Nemanja,
died with this icon on his breast. Its exceptional artistic
qualities of precision and detailed draughtsmanship, its
beauty of colour, modelling and technical perfection,
rank it as one of the most important Serbian icons of
all time and it is believed to have originated in one of
the leading Byzantine icon-painting studios in
Constantinople or Salonika.

Icons

Besides monumental architecture and fresco painting, medieval Serbia also flourished in icon-and miniature-(manuscript) painting and the artistic crafts of metal-working, wood-carving, weaving and embroidery. Icon-painting represents an independent branch of Byzantine art and its artistic approach was closest to, sometimes identical with, that of the monumental painting, developing in parallel with the monumental arts between the 12th and 15th centuries.

According to the rules of the Orthodox Church and iconography, the icon is a portrait. Christ as a man, the Virgin, John the Baptist, the Apostles, the Holy Father of the church and the Christian martyrs and ascetics, all of whom are historical personages, are depicted in a definitive and consistent form.

Panel painting was also known to some earlier civilisations but it was only in the Byzantine time that it assumed a spiritualistic character that was synonymous with Byzantine.

The icon was something more than a commemorative picture. It was the main devotional object of Eastern Christianity and through its sacred matter the believers established an intimate communication with the world of the Lord. Valuable icons are mentioned as the sovereign's gifts to churches and monasteries. They are even mentioned in the biographies of the first Nemanjićs. When describing the building of the rulers' foundation, the author would always mention that the monarch had donated richly framed icons to the church in addition to vessels, books and vestments.

Through the centuries icon painting in Serbia followed all the stages and changes in development of mural paintings. The oldest surviving icons are from the period of the early Nemanjić rulers. Serbian rulers frequently presented icons as gifts to churches abroad. Queen Jelena donated a valuable icon of St Peter and St Paul as a gift to the Vatican and Stefan Dečanski donated the icon of St Nicholas to the church in Bari.

As the centuries passed, the number of icons in Serbian churches grew and later, increasing importance was attached to the iconostasis as a form of art.

We know of only three painters who were Greeks: Nicholas, Manuel and George. They were the so-called 'pictera graeca' and belonged to Kotor's art colony where a renowned school of icon painters grew, producing important works of art, among them the Vatican icon painted before 1314 of St Peter and St Paul with Queen Jelena and her two sons, Dragutin and Milutin.

Hilandar, Mount Athos

The Holy Martyrs - late 14th century. This is the work of an exceptionally gifted artist who worked for several monasteries on Mount Athos. Bright colours and nobility of subject are typical of the epoch. This work is akin to some of the best examples of the contemporaneous Salonika icons. The artist's exuberant lines, the softened an atomical forms and the emphasis on abstract qualities, notably light, are harbingers of the last flowering of Byzantine art before decadence set in with the definitive loss of state sovereignty.

Christ the Pantocrator - icon (1260)
This is one of the most attractive representations of
Christ in late Byzantine art. The anatomically correct
proportioning is further enhanced by a three-dimension-
al sense of volume and exceptional richness of colour.

Hilandar, Mount Athos

The Archangel Gabriel (1360)
This is part of the largest and most important Serbian iconographical work. The artist who painted it also painted for the monastery a large icon to be used in liturgical processions, as well as illuminated manuscripts. He also painted illuminated manuscripts for the other prominent monastery on Mount Athos, Vatopedi.

Hilandar, Mount Athos

above: The Virgin Hodegheria, the most beautiful icon of the 13th century

left: Our Lady of Eloeuse (1293)
From the iconsostasis in the new monastery, Catholicon, donated by King Milutin in 1293, together with its sister icon, the icon of Christ the Pantocrator, this is the largest icon at Hilandar. Notwithstanding its size, the figure has been defined by very fine brushstrokes. The icon was originally sheathed in silver. A partial re-painting of Christ's robes is noticeable, dating from the original time of painting.

right: The Virgin with Three Hands
This is the most venerated of icons at Hilandar. This icon has shown miraculous powers by healing the hand of St John of Damascus, who was ironically opposed to iconoclasm. As his hand healed St John added an extra hand to the icon in gratitude.
   The icon is moulded in silver and coated afterwards. According to the legend, the icon was brought to Europe from Jerusalem by St Sava.

Dečani Treasuries

High Dečani has the richest treasures of all monasteries in Serbia. The numerous gifts were donated by the royal founders, Stefan Dečanski and his son, the Emperor Dušan The treasury is best known for its collection of icons and some of these are of great artistic value. The most valuable icons are from the original stone iconostasis painted by the same masters who painted the frescoes in the church in 1348. The icons of Christ, the Virgin, John the Baptist, St Nicholas and the Archangel Gabriel rank among the best works of Serbian medieval icon painting.

opposite page

top/left: Christ

bottom/left: The Virgin and a Playful Christ

right: Archangel Gabriel

this page
The Stefan Dečanski icon.
The most important icons were painted in the second part of the 16th century by the sinner-artist Longin, one of the best Serbian fresco and icon painters in Dečani, showing scenes from Dečanski's early life, based on the early 15th century hagiography written by Grigorije Camblak.

There are twenty-three crucifixes in the church treasury and two are especially valuable; the Stefan Dečanski cross and the Emperor Dušan cross, made in gilded silver and decorated with precious stones.

right: The Stefan Dečanski cross

above left: Grand Duke Jovan Oliver, fresco, Lesnovo
The church of Lesnovo was built in 1341 by Grand Duke Jovan Oliver, who was given the title of Despot some time later by Emperor Dušan. The subject-matter is usual: the Pantocrator and the Divine Liturgy in the dome, the Great Feasts, the Passion and Christ's miracles and parables on the walls. The church's most striking fresco is a portrait of the founder Despot Oliver, in rich aristocratic robes and with the model of the church in his hand.

above right: Marko's Monastery
The construction of the church began in 1345 during the time of Emperor Dušan and it was completed in the time of King Marko after whom it was named. The frescoes were painted in the eighth decade of the 14th century and their iconography is based on religious poetry. The expansion of this art was not followed by an equal improvement in quality. New themes, each more dramatic than the last, appeared everywhere, but painting itself became increasingly provincial. It had lost all sense of proportion, becoming violent and extreme: the pathos was exaggerated and faces were distorted.

right: St Basil, fresco, Marko's Monastery.

After King Stefan Dečanski was dethroned and imprisoned by his son Dušan and shortly afterwards strangled, Stefan Dušan, usually known as Tsar Dušan, became the new Serbian ruler. Medieval Serbia reached the zenith of its power during his reign. On Easter Day 1345 he had himself crowned Emperor of the Serbs and the Greeks. By that time he had many Greek subjects living in the areas he had conquered from the Byzantine emperor.

Dušan's empire

Shortly after his coronation, the archbishop of Serbia was upgraded to a patriarch. During Tsar Dušan's reign, and even before, the high dignitaries of the state also became entitled to build churches. Thus a considerable number of pious foundations were erected. In nearly all, the style of the well known Serbian painters and their followers continued.

Churches built by the nobility, who followed the examples set by their sovereigns, were a novelty in this period. Their construction led to a still greater increase in fresco paintings, while it led to a new stage in secular painting, when the portraits of nobles, their wives, children and grandchildren first appeared.

Dušan's empire was short-lived. After a prolonged succession of conflicts, Dušan was succeeded by his son Uroš (Stefan Uroš V). During the latter's reign the empire disintegrated, a process begun by Dušan's half-brother Simeon, who proclaimed himself "Tsar of all the Greeks, Serbs and all Albanians and who reigned until 1359. There were other provincial rulers who did the same, among them the brothers Vukašin and Uglješa in Macedonia. Vukašin assumed the title of King in 1366. Both brothers campaigned against the Ottoman Turks, who first appeared in the Balkans in the 1340s. Both were killed at the battle of Marica River, where the Serbs sustained a terrible defeat. As a direct result of this battle, Turkish power was effectively established in Macedonia. A famous, half-legendary personality belonging to this unhappy period of Balkan history was Vukašin's son Kraljević Marko "the Little King"; he was a kind of Balkan Robin Hood, whose adventures and exploits form the basis of many epic songs in Serbian national poetry.

Tsar Uroš died in 1371 and the centre of the Serbian state was moved northwards to the region ruled by Prince Lazar Hrebeljanović. By making prudent and far-reaching strategic moves, Prince Lazar soon rose above the other lords to impose himself as Nemanja's successor and what remained of Dušan's empire passed over to him. He was connected to the Nemanjić dynasty by marriage. The area he ruled was small and he assumed the modest title of Prince, establishing his capital at Kruševac, where he carried out an ambitious building programme.

Prince Lazar acquired an enviable reputation when he united the Church of Serbia and Constantinople, whereby the Serbian religious head was finally recognised as a patriarch. Besides Prince Lazar, there were other prominent Serbian lords that Prince Lazar had neither the time nor the might to subjugate and thus the unification of the Serbian state was not possible. All his attempts to create a unified Serbian state was stopped by the Turks. It was Prince Lazar who led the Serbian army at the battle of Kosovo.

The Battle of Kosovo

The Battle of Kosovo

The two armies formally met on St Vitus' Day, 15 June 1389. The Serbs lost most of their nobility, a large part of their army and the country came to the brink of total catastrophe. The battle of Kosovo has become one of the great paradoxes of history because, although victory went to the Turks, marking the first stage in the Turkish conquest of the Serbs, in the folk history of the Serbs, defeat was transmitted into a spiritual victory and regarded as a source of pride rather than humiliation. Prince Lazar and Miloš later became cult figures of the Kosovo legend.

In the period after Tsar Uroš V, the building of churches continued. King Marko spared no effort to finish the church built in 1346-47 by his father Vukašin. The paintings in the church were finished in 1376-77 and the church was named Marko's Monastery. The scenes painted in the church are mainly illustrations of liturgical songs and complicated theological themes. The painters introduced some innovations; they portrayed excitement in the use of sharp contrasts of light which added drama and mystery to the paintings, this was also done by using unusual harmonies of colour.

It is interesting how the artists approached certain arrangements using colour and their feelings of pictorial values to make paintings look quite modern. These frescoes are imbued with a realism which occasionally turns into naturalism.

In 1389, the year of the disastrous battle of Kosovo, the little church of St Andrew was built and decorated. The frescoes were painted by Bishop Jovan and his assistant Grigorije (a name given to monks down the centuries), and the signature of the zograf (icon painter) is still significantly legible. The provincial frescoes of St Andrews recapture, to some extent, the monumental past. Art and life of the spirit survived longer than political power but paintings were by now only an echo of past splendours.

The Battle of Kosovo by A Stefanović (National Museum of Belgrade)

opposite: The Feudal States before the Battle of Kosovo

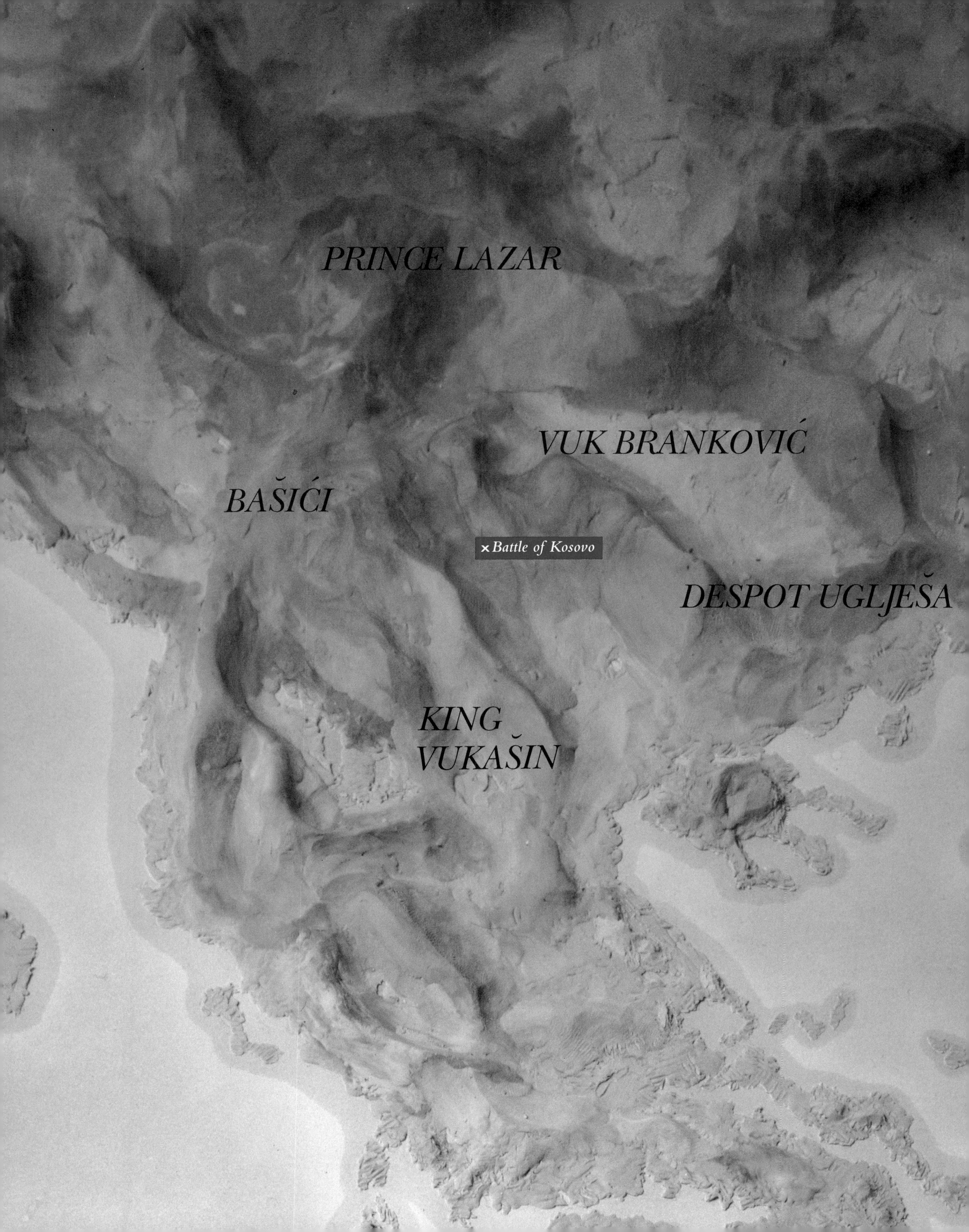

PRINCE LAZAR

VUK BRANKOVIĆ

BAŠIĆI

✕ *Battle of Kosovo*

DESPOT UGLJEŠA

KING
VUKAŠIN

The Serbian bards composed cycles of poems concerning Prince Lazar, Princess Milica and the Battle of Kosovo:

The Kosovo Girl

The Kosovo girl wakes early
Wakes early on a Sunday,
On a Sunday before the bright sun:
She rolls up her white sleeves,
She rolls them back to the white elbows,
She carries white bread on her shoulder,
And in her hands she has jugs of gold,
She has one jug of cold water,
She has one jug of red red wine.
She makes her way to Kosovo meadow,
A young girl to walk the battlefield,
The battlefield of the honoured prince.
She turns the heroes over in their blood,
And every hero she finds alive,
She washes the hero in cold water,
She gives the sarcament of red wine,
She gives him the white bread to eat,
And fortune fell on the hero,
On Pavle Orlovich, the young man
Who carried the Prince's battlestandard:
And she discovered him alive
And his right hand had been cut off,
And his left leg cut off at the knee,
And his supple ribs were in fragments,
His liver showing pale;

She took him from the floods of his blood
She washed him in the coldness of water,
And she gave him the sacrament of red wine,
She gives him white bread to eat.
And the hero's heart began to dance
And Pavle Orlovich is speaking:
"Kosovo girl, my darling sister
What troubles you so terribly
That you turn over heroes in their blood?
Young girl walking the battlefield,
Who are you looking for?
Is it your brother, your cousin?
Or is it your old father, God forgive him?"

The Kosovo girl said:
"My darling brother, soldier I do not know,
I am not looking for my family,
It is not my brother, it is not my cousin,
It is not my father, God forgive him.
But you could know, soldier I do not know,
When Lazar the Lord with his army
Took the sacrament together,
At the wonderful church of the Almighty,
With thirty monks for three weeks of days
The Serbian army took the sacrament,

And three dukes at the end, lords of war.
And the first is Milosh the Duke,
And the second is Ivan Kosanchich,
And the third one is Milan Toplitsa.

I was standing there in the gates
When Milosh the Duke walked out,
An honourable hero in this world,
Trailing a long sword on the cobbled road,
With a silk handkerchief around his neck,
And capped· in silk and feathers set in silver,
And long tunic embroidered in circles.
Then turning where I was and seeing me,
He took his tunic off and gave me it:
"Here young girl, my tunic with circles,
And you shall remember me by this,
By my tunic and by my name.
Look my dear, I am on my way to die,
In the battle-camp of the Glorious Prince,
O my dear, pray to God
I may come home to you safe from my regiment
And good luck shall come on you also:
And I will take you for my Milan's wife,
For Milan my brother in God,
Who named me by God his brother,

192

By the most high God and by Saint John,
And I will hold the crown at your wedding."

Ivan Kosanchich came after him
An honourable hero in this world,
Trailing a long sword on the cobbled road,
And capped in silk and feathers set in silver,
And a tunic embroidered in circles,
And a handkerchief of silk around his neck,
And a gilded ring on his hand
He turned where I was and he saw me,
He gave the ring from his own hand:
"Here young girl, my gilded ring,
And you shall remember me by this,
By my ring and by my name.
Look, my dear, I am on my way to die,
In the battle-camp of the glorious Prince,
And, O my dear, pray to God
I may come home to you safe from my regiment
And good luck shall come on you also:
And I will take you for Milan's wife,
For Milan my brother in God,
Who named me by God his brother,
By the most high God and by Saint John,
And I will lead you in at your wedding."

Milan Toplitsa came after him,
An honourable hero in this world,
Trailing a long sword on the cobbled road,
And capped in silk and feathers set in silver,
And a tunic embroidered in circles,
And a handkerchief of silk round his neck,
Over his hand a scarf embroidered in gold.
He turned where I was and he saw me,
He drew the scarf of gold from his own hand,
He took it from his hand and he gave me it:
"Here, young girl, my gold-embroidered scarf,
And you shall remember me by this,
By my scarf and by my name.
Look, my dear, I am on my way to die,
In the battle-camp of the glorious Prince,
And, O my dear, pray to God
I may come home to you safe from my regiment
And good luck shall come on you, my dear,
And I will take you for my faithful love."

And the three dukes, the lords of war, went;
Now I look for them! on the battlefield."
And Pavle Orlovich said:
"Kosovo girl, my darling sister,
Look, my dear, at the battle-lances,

Where they are so tall and so dense:
That is where the blood of the heroes bled,
Stirrup-iron deep to a high horse,
Stirrup-iron deep and girth deep,
And deep as the silk belts on fighting-men.
And that is where those three died.
Go home now to your whitewashed house,
With an unbloody hem, unbloody sleeve."
And when the young girl heard his words
She dropped tears down on her white face,
She went away to her whitewashed house,
And her white throat lamented:
"Unhappy! Evil luck has come on me.
Unhappy, if I were to grasp a green pine,
Even the green pine would wither."

193

The Downfall of the Serbian Empire

Flying hawk, grey bird,
Out of the holy place, out of Jerusalem,
Holding a swallow, holding a bird.
That is no hawk, grey bird,
That is Elijah, holy one;
Holding no swallow, no bird,
But writing from the Mother of God
To the Emperor at Kosovo.

He drops that writing on his knee,
It is speaking to the Emperor:
"Lazar, glorious Emperor,
Which is the empire of your choice?
Is it the empire of heaven?
Is it the empire of the earth?

If it is the empire of the earth,
Saddle horses and tighten girth-straps,
And, fighting-men, buckle on swords,
Attack the Turks,
And all the Turkish army shall die.

But if the empire of heaven
Leave a church on Kosovo,
Build its foundation not with marble stones,
Build it with pure silk and with crimson cloth,
Take the Sacrament, marshal the men,
They shall all die,
And you shall die among them as they die.

And when the Emperor heard those words
He considered and thought:
"Kind God what shall I do, how shall I do it?
What is the empire of my choice?
Is it the empire of heaven?
Is it the empire of the earth?
And if I shall choose the empire
And choose the empire of the earth,
The empire of the earth is brief,
Heaven is lasting and everlasting.
And the Emperor chose the empire of heaven
Above the empire of the earth.

He built a church on Kosovo,
Built its foundation not of marble stone,
But with pure silk and with crimson cloth.
He called for the Patriarch of Serbia,
He called for the twelve great bishops,
He took the Sacrament with his men;
And when when the prince
Had marshalled his men,
The Turkish army struck at Kosovo.

Jug Bogdan the Old moves his army
With his nine sons the nine Jugovichi,
Nine grey hawks, grey birds,
Every one has nine thousand men.
Jug has twelve thousand men,
Beating and slashing at the Turks.
They battled, they slaughtered seven pashas,
They battled with the eighth pasha,
And Jug Bogdan the Old was killed,
And the nine Jugovichi were killed,
Nine grey hawks, grey birds,
And all of their men were killed.

The three Merljavchevichi move their men,
The Ban Ugljesha, Gojko the Duke,
Vukashing the King,
Every one has thirty thousand men,
Beating and slashing at the Turks
They battled, they slaughtered eight pashas,
They battled with the ninth pasha,
The two Merjavchevichi were killed,
The Ban Ugljesha, Gojko the Duke,
Vukashin dropped loaded with wounds,
Turkish horses trampled him under,
And all of their men were killed.

The Herzog Stephen moves his men,
His force is strong and great sixty thousand
A great army beating and slashing at the Turks
They battled, they slaughtered nine pashas
They battled with the tenth pasha,
The Herzog Stephen was killed
And all of his men were killed.

Lazar, Prince of Serbia, moved his men.
Lazar had Serbs without number,
Seven and seventy thousand men,
Hunting the Turks across Kosovo,
Moving too swiftly to be seen by them.
And how could there be battle with the Turks.
God be the death of Vuk Brankovich
Traitor to his kinsmen on Kosovo:
The Turks dragged down Lazar,
Lazar, Prince of Serbia was killed
And all of his men were killed,
Seven and seventy thousand men:
With holiness and honour
Good in the sight of God.

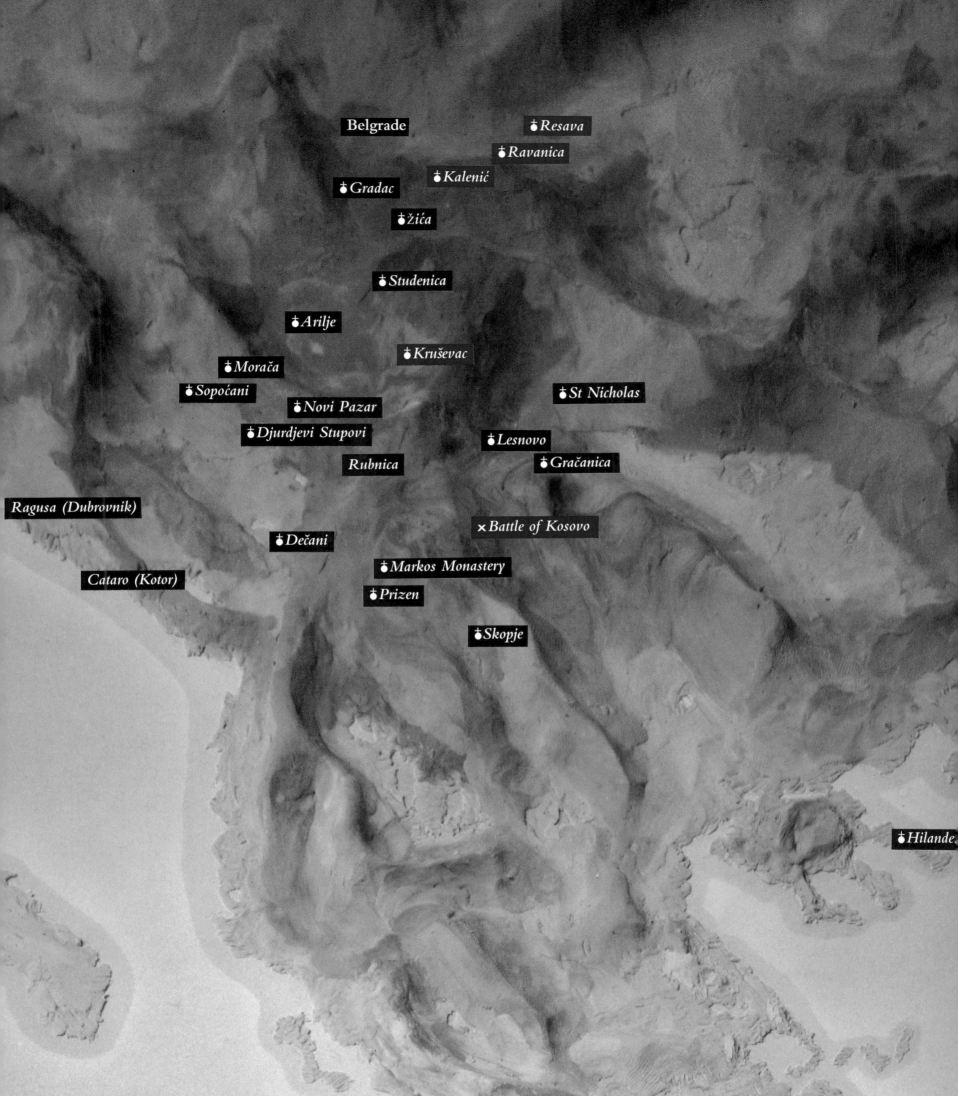

Belgrade ⚭ Resava

⚭ Ravanica

⚭ Kalenić

⚭ Gradac

⚭ Žiča

⚭ Studenica

⚭ Arilje

⚭ Kruševac

⚭ Morača

⚭ Sopoćani ⚭ St Nicholas

⚭ Novi Pazar

⚭ Djurdjevi Stupovi ⚭ Lesnovo

Rubnica ⚭ Gračanica

Ragusa (Dubrovnik)

✕ Battle of Kosovo

⚭ Dečani

⚭ Markos Monastery

Cataro (Kotor)

⚭ Prizen

⚭ Skopje

⚭ Hilande.

Chapter four

THE MORAVA SCHOOL

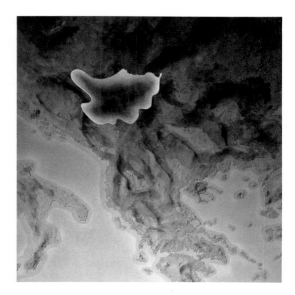

Serbia after the Battle of Kosovo

After the battle of Kosovo, the great Serbian state was severely reduced in size. It was also one of the last Christian states in the Balkans. Prince Lazar's successor, his son Despot Stefan Lazarević (1389-1402 and 1402-27), retreated before the Turks. With the help of his mother, Princess Milica, he strove hard to establish order in the new principality around the Morava river and save the Serbian state. He achieved what had seemed to be the impossible and gained international prestige (he was both Turkish vassal and Hungarian palatine since 1402).

He worked on internal relations within the principality, founded and improved the central administration, giving him control over the subordinated nobility; and built new fortifications, monasteries and churches. Despot Stefan Lazarević was a patron of the arts and a man of letters. He was the last representative of the knights' dying era and also heralded the new renaissance period.

Life at the court of the Despot Stefan was characterised by the same luxury and ceremony of everyday life, with religion and the arts, as was enjoyed by his equals in the West. He enjoyed reading, took part in tournaments and other knights' gatherings and entertainments and left his personal imprint on his time through an art that was both elegant and luxurious.

His principality became the refuge of the most eminent people of letters, scholars, monks and feudal lords who, having lost their own lands, brought with them the best Byzantine, Bulgarian and one-time Serbian traditions.

Literature

Literacy flourished, thanks to the great number of Serbian, Bulgarian and Greek monks arriving in Serbia from Mount Athos, who copied and translated important works. Renowned writers and historians, e.g. Grigorije Camblak (Stefan Dečanski's biographer), Constantine the Philosopher (Despot Stefan's biographer and reformer of Resava orthography) continued their fruitful work in Serbia. The Byzantine poets Antonije Epactit and Dimitrise Cantazune also chanted in their works praise of the Serbia of their time.

Literature of the 14th century and the beginning of the 15th century produced rare value and led to the development of new genres and stylistic forms. It was a new epoch, the so-called Kosovo cycle of the Old Serbian literature. Large numbers of works dedicated to the battle of Kosovo, to the glory of the Great Martyr, Prince Lazar, and the Serbian hero of Kosovo, Miloš Obilić.

Jefimija, the unhappy widow of one of the Serbian nobles killed in the battle of Marica, fled to Serbia, where she found refuge at the court of Prince Lazar, to whom she was distantly related. After Prince Lazar was killed at the battle of Kosovo, Jefimija sought shelter in the convent and became a nun, composing a eulogy to her kinsman and protector. This was not written on parchment or paper but embroidered on a shroud for Prince Lazar on which was represented the work of vanquished Serbdom. It must be one of the saddest and most moving samplers ever produced.

Now that thou hast departed to eternal joy
Thy children are sunk in pain and sorrow
For they are under the rule of the infidel
And all need thy help.

So we pray thee to offer thy prayers to the faith
Ruler for thy children
And for all who serve them with love and faith
For they are cast down in great affliction.

Those who eat their bread have plotted against them
And thy good are forgotten, thou holy martyr.
If thou hast passed beyond this life
Yet thou knowest the pain and misery of thy children

And as a holy martyr thou hast free access to the Lord.

Serbian literature did not cease to live, although the Serbian state had been reduced in size so drastically. Aside from works glorifying the struggle for national consciousness, there were also poetic works. Despot Stefan himself was a writer, composing a species of lyric poem, Slovo Ljubve (A song of love), a poetic epistle and a hymn to spiritual love.

above: examples of Morava style architecture, from Ravanica monastery

Architecture

Brought to an end by the arrival of the Turks in the Balkans at the end of the 14th century, this grand epoch produced architecture of great originality, almost essentially Serbian. By this time the old Serbians had freed themselves from the Roman and Byzantine influences and elaborated a new type of construction and decoration based on an almost original concept. This new style of building is called the Morava style or the Morava school.

The monuments in the Morava style were built during the reign of Prince Lazar, his son Despot Stefan Lazarević and Despot Djuradj Branković. Though the Morava style did not last long, its monasteries and churches have nevertheless made it famous. The basic plan of the churches is still in the form of an 'inscribed cross' either with a single cupola or five cupolas but in combination with the trefoil 'triconical' plan. The exterior line of the three apses is pentagonal, the cupolas of the church are often raised higher on the square socle. Their facades are characterised by alternating rows of bricks - one row of stone, three of bricks - separated by a thick layer of mortar, and by the use of rich carvings around the doors and windows. Elaborate and delicately carved stone rosettes placed in the centre of the chess-board on the upper level, are also typical of the Morava facades. The sculptures of animals are chiselled in limestone and they remain very much a part of the ornamentation on Oriental churches.

In the last decade of the 14th century and the beginning of the 15th, the Morava style reached its climax in Serbia, where rather peculiar forms of the body of the church were decorated and constructed in a manner not seen anywhere else.

Through its achievements, Serbian medieval architecture has secured a deserved place in the general history of the world of art. It deserves its place by virtue of being an independent artistic group, with distinctive features in its fundamental concept and its original spirit by its peculiar style and details.

The most representative monuments of the Morava style are the Lazarica church in Ravanica, Kalenić and Manasija (Resava).

Paintings

Morava art of that time had an aristocratic character, having originated in the despot's court and the courts of his lords. The paintings reflect the wealth and abundance of luxury in the almost Oriental ornaments, gold, silk, costly cobalt and, above all, the elegance of the appointed subjects. The new style of the Morava school is distinguished mainly by the return to the monumental forms which now acquired a somewhat decorative character. The drawing is fluent, the colouring refined and lavish, the movements of the figures elegant and daring. They introduced purity of the form, flexibility of the line, a harmony of carefully selected colours and iconographical beauty of modelling.

This new concept of Morava painting is marked by a more natural relationship between figures and the architecture or landscape around them. New also was the decorative system of the disposition of the paintings on the walls, i.e. the holy warriors and saints are represented in the medallions and decorated by plated rainbow colours.

In describing the biblical scenes the painters understandably clothed their subject in the apparel and in the settings of their own time, giving us valuable information. This was an art of the soft, lyrical feelings and rich inner life of a civilisation endowed with refined taste, yet threatened by death. These paintings brought new beauty in such great quantity that the experts thought that it could only have originated on Serbian soil.

The frescoes of the monasteries at Ravanica, Kalenić and Resava end the great medieval chapter of Serbian art.

Ravanica - *Architecture*
This is one of the most beautiful examples of Morava school architecture. It is a five-domed trefoil in plan. The central dome is quite large. The combination of hewn stone and brick produces a very decorative effect: the outer walls are divided into three bands of horizontal belt course, the window arches in the middle and upper bands featuring elaborate stonework. The large rosette on the west facade and pointed panels on the drums of the small cupolas added further decoration.

Ravanica - *Paintings*

*The earliest frescoes in Ravanica were painted in the
14th century tradition. They are in the central dome
(Christ Pantocrator, the divine Liturgy and sixteen
prophets) but they are not innovative. The most
famous paintings, which made Ravenica so well
known,*
occupy the outer surfaces of the main part of the church.

*These frescoes are ornamented in gold and azure, very
powerful and original in style and the beginning of the
Morava style in painting. Scenes depicting Christ's
miracles, and the characteristic medallions with saints'
portraits in a full colour range appear for the first time.*

*The most remarkable compositions in Ravanica are
Christ's entry into Jerusalem and the Healing of the
Blind (left), the Warrior Saints (right) and portraits of
Prince Lazar and Princess Milica and their sons,
Stefan and Vuk. They rank among the masterpieces of
Byzantine art of the latter part of the 14th century.*

Ravanica -Warrior Saints - fresco (details)
The motif of the Holy Warriors is already an
important subject for painters of the Ravanica
monastery, where they insisted on emphasising the
youthfulness of the figures, endowing them with a
lyric, almost feminine, sensibility.

Kalenić - *Architecture*
The monastery at Levac, dedicated to the Virgin Mary. The church has a trefoil ground plan with semi-circular choir chapels in the north and south walls. The main octagonal dome is decorated with a painted chequered pattern.

The beauty of the facade owes much to the bas-relief carving around the two light windows and portals. The church was constructed of alternating layers of dressed stone and brick. The decoration of the church was emphasised by the use of rose windows.

The sculpture, painted decoration and lavishly ornamented portals are distinctive features of Kalenić architecture.

Frescoes

These frescoes, dating from 1413, rank among the highest achievements of the Morava school. The Communion of the Apostles and the Procession of the Church Fathers have been preserved in the apse, and imago pietatis is in the prothesis. In the nave are the standing figures of warriors and saints, while scenes from the life of the Virgin are in the narthex.

The characteristic of the frescoes is the harmonious use of colour, particularley in the frescoe of the Miracle at Cana and the Miracle of the Loaves and Fishes. The Kalenič monastery is considered one of the most important cultural monuments of the Morava school.

Resava (or Manasija)

The monastery and the fortification around the monastery were constructed between 1407 and 1418 during the reign of Despot Stefan Lazarević. In the first half of the 15th century Constantin the Philosopher, an author of the biography of Despot Stefan, wrote that the monastery was the most important Serbian cultural centre, in which books were copied and translated and the Serbian language style was polished. He also wrote that Stefan in his youth had once said, while watching the construction of churches, "I'll build a bigger and more beautiful church." He travelled extensively throughout the land and looked for the most beautiful appropriate place to build; finally he selected the picturesque site of Resava.

Architecture

The church surpasses all the Morava-style buildings of Serbia. It is a five-domed church with a trefoil ground plan, its large central dome supported by four great piers with engaged colonnades. A long, elegant frieze running above the arcades adds a special note to the architectural design, typical of Romanesque and Gothic styles.

Resava - *Paintings*

The frescoes in the monastery are a brilliant synthesis of Byzantine and Western art, which continued the rich artistic tradition of medieval Serbia. There are compositions of scenes of Christ's Miracles, the parables of the rich and poor, Lazar, the emperor's wedding, the prodigal son, the Pharisee and other scenes from the life of Christ.

The Assumption of the Virgin, on the west wall of the central dome, includes images of the prophets, and groups of warriors. Saints in splendid gilded robes and armour are in the lower zone. The Divine Liturgy in the altar and busts of saints in medallions are in dazzling colours of gold and azure. Large portraits of the founder, Despot Stefan, holding a model of the church in one hand, on the west wall, are the best compositions in the Resava church.

Resava
far left: The Holy Warriors - Aretos, Nestor and Nikita (detail left)
The Holy Warriors on the wall of Resava were to remain the last knightly farewell of the Balkans to troubadour Europe.

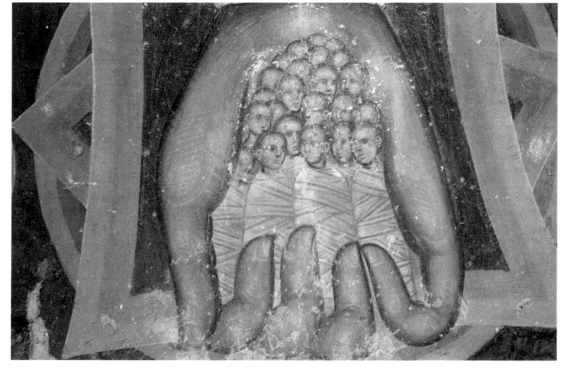

Resava

above far left: The Emperor's feast

above right: St Peter of Alexandria

left: Souls in the Lord's Hand

above: The Apostles' Communion

Resava

left: St Mercurius the Warrior

right: The saint from Medallion

215

Resava
above: The parable of Poor Lazarus (detail)

right: St Sylvester, Roman Pope

217

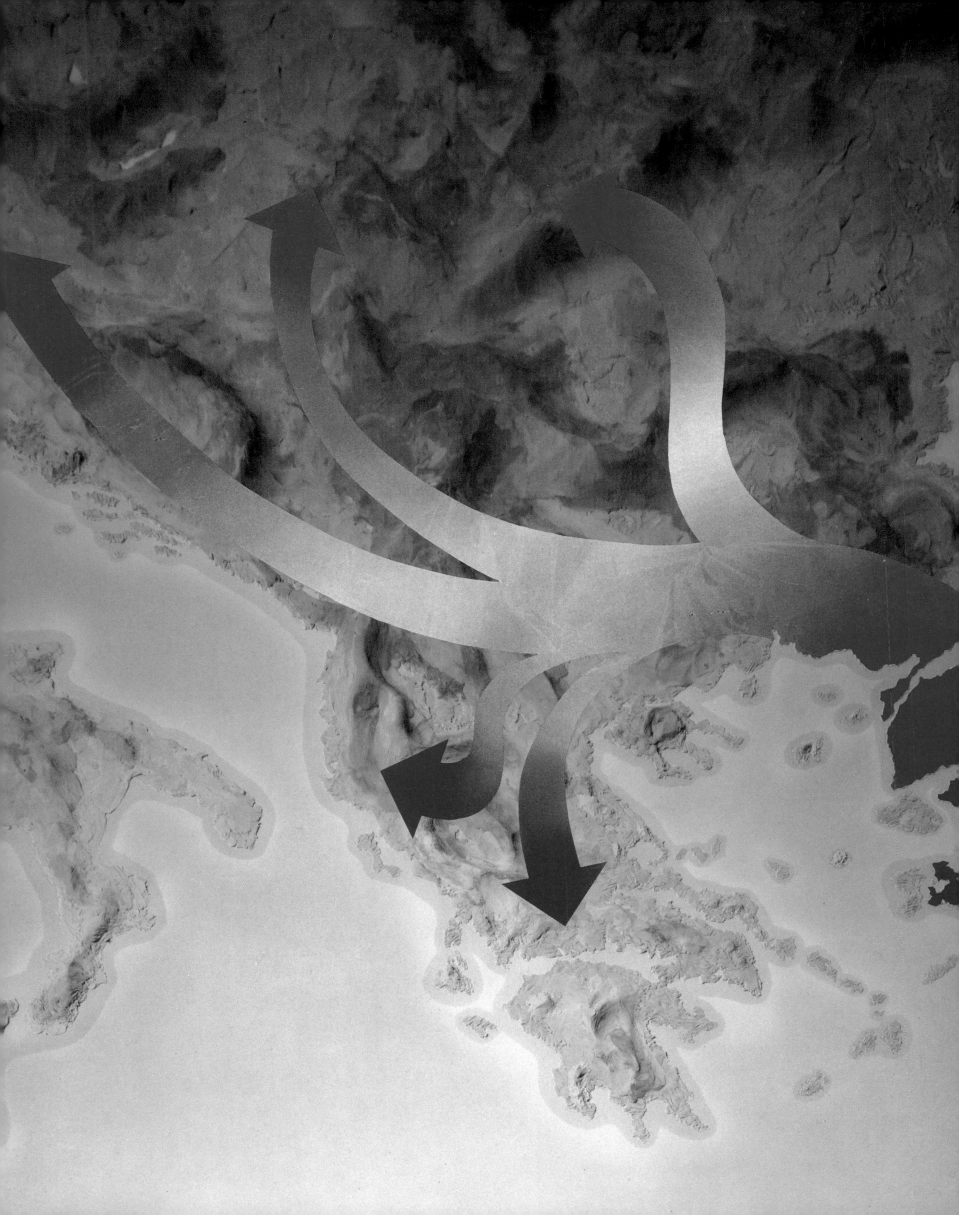

SERBIA UNDER THE TURKS

Opposite: The Turkish Conquest

The last free Balkan states were conquered by the Turks during the second half of the 15th century. Constantinople fell in 1453, Serbia in 1459, Montenegro in 1499; Belgrade was the last to fall in 1521 and the Serbian Church lost its independence between 1525 and 1528.

Under Turkish rule Serbia was divided into Ottoman administrative units: Sanjaks, Kadiliks and Nahiyes. The Serbian ruling class, the feudal lords, learned people and monks, mostly fled the country or were killed, though there were some who agreed to co-operate with the Turks. The land and the income of the feudal lords came into the Sultan's hands and the property was divided into timars (Turkish feudal states) and given to the spahis (Turkish warriors).

The Turkish conquest was followed by large-scale movements of the Serbian population. Masses of fugitives fled Serbia and within a century Serbs found themselves scattered over large areas far from home. They reached Dalmatia, Croatia, Slavonia and distant parts of Hungary. The Hapsburg rulers of the remaining Croatian and Hungarian lands systematically settled Serbs there as a protection against Ottoman incursions. The former land of the Serbs, having been left ravaged and deserted, were now populated by Vlachs from the mountain regions. The towns, always ethnically mixed, were being increasingly inhabited by Turks. The Turks destroyed every document concerning Serbian National life in order to force Serbian people to be obedient. Forced conversion to Islam brought a section of the population close to the conqueror. The rest of the Serbs devoted themselves to their lands and living a patriarchal way of life in the remote villages.

For more than four centuries the Serbs were divided between two rival empires, Turkey and Austria. The separation was bridged by historical tradition preserved through epic songs and by the Orthodox Church. In 1557 the Patriarch of Peć (the centre of the Serbian Orthodox Church) was restored.

The Serbs south of the rivers Sava and Danube now consisted of peasants; there were also monks, tradesmen and craftsmen, who gradually became rich. During the Ottoman occupation they organised uprisings which caused new ravages and migrations. Serbs managed to gain independence of the Patriarch of Peć in 1557 and the Serbian Orthodox Church became the faithful keeper of its cultural heritage, whose history and arts they glorified in legends and folk poetry. The Church played an important role in the renewal of the tradition and the promotion of the arts.

The Patriarchy of Peć and Dečani became centres of scholarship. Patriarchs, abbots and the rich peasants and craftsmen commissioned works of art. Most often the work was produced by gifted, self-taught, local people, rather than by painters from Constantinople and Salonika. As they could not produce the high standard of the paintings of their predecessors they became very skilful copycats.

Still, Serbian 16th century art had its most important painter, Monk Longin, who was a writer, poet, illuminator of church books and painter of frescoes and icons. Longin travelled round Serbia, covering vast areas and for thirty-five years painted churches and monasteries. He painted the narthex in the Patriarchy of Peć, frescoes in Studenica and Mileševa, worked in Gračanica and painted the icons at Dečani and the iconostasis at the monastery of Piva. He also painted the most grandiose icon, his finest work, in which he presented the king and scenes from the life of Stefan Dečanski after a biography written by Grigorije Camblak. He wrote the text to Stefan Dečanski: "I beseech thee to intercede with Christ our Lord for me, His humble servant, who with my hand and soul have painted this and offered to you with love, I, unworthy servant of Christ, Longin, monk and painter." There were other painters who carried out work in Serbia. In the 17th century Patriarch Pajsije, a man interested in church affairs and art, travelled constantly, taking care to protect and preserve old churches and monasteries. He also copied and bound books himself. He was a monk and painter who came from Hilandar monastery. He was very well acquainted with the Italo-Cretan art style and he transferred it to Serbian soil.

Opposite: Scenes from the life of Stefan Dečanski

St Nicholas – King Stefan Dečanski and his wife donated this icon to the Cathederal of St Nicholas in Bari.

After the collapse of the Serbian despotism (1759), the kingdom of Bosnia (1463) and Hecegovina (1481) Montenegro, a land of high and impassable mountains, was able to hold off the Turks until 1492 when it eventually fell to the Ottoman empire.

The Turkish Sultan entrusted all the conquered land to spahis and the Serbs themselves were bound slaves. In the beginning the taxes which the Serbian peasants had to pay to the Turks were not high, but the spahis started to change the rules over the states and in time the imposed taxes increased in number and amount, worsening the peasants, position. The most painful tax was 'blood tax' when every five years the Turks selected the best non-Muslim children for the regular army (called the Janizary). Some Serbian children were educated in the Turkish way and even became distinguished personalities at the Sultan's court.

Mehmed Paša Sokolović, Serb by birth, became a Grand Vizier during the reign of Sultan Suleyman II, and rose to the highest position among those Serbs who had adopted Islamic manners. It was with Mehmed Paša's help and influence that Suleyman II issued a decree restoring the Serbian church and re-establishing the Patriarch of Peć The Serbs became united under the Patriarch, and the orthodox religion was the only faith that merged the whole of the spiritual heritage of the Serbian people, becoming a vehicle for Serbian national ideology.

The Period of re-establishment of the Patriarchate of Peć marked the revival of the spiritual and cultural life of Serbia. Dečani, Gračanica and the Patriarchate of Peć once again became cultural centres.

The churches were rebuilt and new churches were built by native builders who had added new parvises to the old monasteries. The churches were decorated and painted by native painters who also made new frescoes and icons. The monks copied old manuscripts, wrote and illuminated new religious books and biographies. It was during this period that the first printing press was established in the monastery of Gračanica.

Icon of the Apostles Peter and Paul – donated by Queen Jelena, wife of King Uroš, with her sons Dragutin and Milutin (the original icon is currently in the Vatican).

St Sava and St Simeon
Another painter, known as Cosma, worked in Serbia.
This gifted artist copied the iconographical schemes
painted by Longin, but he also brought to Serbian
paintings of the period tremendous coloristic force.

Migration by Paja Jovanović

The Migration of the Serbs

From the second half of the 16th century, the situation in Serbia changed tremendously. Some of the janizaries slowly occupied the highest positions in Serbia and they took the law into their own hands, becoming the worst enemies and persecutors of the Christian Serbs.

Life soon became intolerable for them and the great migration across the rivers Sava and Danube began, headed by the Patriarch Arsenije Carnojevic, with Serbian nobles, monks and dignitaries taking as many religious treasures as possible from Peć.

About 37,000 Serbian families (185,000 Serbs) left Serbia. Serbian towns and villages ceased to exist, leaving the Turks and Albanians (converted Muslims) to devastate the monasteries and churches.

The Hapsburg Empire welcomed the Serbs and the Viennese court granted them privileges in the form of guarantees of freedom of religious practice, church autonomy and even the right to elect bodies of local government.

They started building churches and monasteries, opened schools and started a new life, accepting the European artistic and cultural trends of their new surroundings. But they continued to fight for the re-establishment of despotism in the following decades, and for a long time felt themselves to be aliens, deprived of their homeland.

Bibliography

Babić, G   Kraljeva Crkva u Studenici, Beograd 1986.

Beckwith, J   Early Christian and Byzantine Art, London 1970.

Benn, Dr E   Yugoslavia part one, The history of the Yugoslav lands up
                  to the outbreak of the First World War.

Beograd, Srbiji   Istorija srpskog naroda, I,II, Beograd 1981.
                  Zadužbine Kosova, Prizren – Beograd 1989.

Bogdonović, D   Istorija srpske književnosti, Beograd 1980.

Ćirković, S   Studenica Monastery, Belgrade 1986.

Ćurić, S &   Gračanica istorija i arhitektura, Beograd 1988.
Heppell, M

Ćurićić, S   Gračanica – King Milutin's Church and its place in late
                  Byzantine Architecture, Pennsylvania State University 1979.

Deroko, A   Monumentalna, dekorativna arhitektura u srednjcvekovnoj
                  Srbiji, Beograd 1962.

Djurić, V   Ikone svetoga kralja Stepfana Dečanskog, Beograd 1985.
                  Treasures of Yugoslavia, Beograd 1980.
                  Illustrated History of the Serbs, Beograd 1991, I-IV vol.
                  Srednjovekovna umjetnost Srba. Zagreb 1985.
                  Studenica, souvenir, Beograd 1991.
                  Sopoćani, Beograd 1991.

Djurić, V J   Icouse de Yugoslavie, Belgrade 1961.

Jackson, T G   Serbian Church architecture, London 1918.

Kašanin, M   Manastir Studenica, Beograd 1986.

Ljubinković, M   Le Monastére de Ravanica, Beograd 1989.
                  Cirilo i Metodije, Beograd 1964.

Marinković, R   Iz naše književnosti feudalnog doba, Beograd 1959.

Mijović, P   Art Treasures of Montenegro, Beograd 1980.

Milošević, D   Gračanica Monastery, Beograd 1989.

Mirković, l   Crkvene starine iz Dečana, Peći, Cetinja, i Praskavice.
                  Godišnjak Muzeja Južne Srbije, Knj I. Skopje 1937.

Muller, P   Famous frescoes, Munich 1986.

Petković, S   Zidno slikarstvo na području Pećke Patrijarsije
                  1557 – 1614, Novi Sad 1965.

Radojčić, Dj Sp Istorijski razvoj srpske rukopsne i štampane, knjige.
       Beograd 1952.

Radojčić, S   Stare srpske minijature, Beograd 1950.
       The Golden Age of Wall Painting, Boston 1962.
       Ikone Makedonije i Srbije, Beograd 1966.

Radojčić, S &   Majstori starog srpskog slikarstva, Beograd 1952.
Pavićić, Dr D

Radojković, B   Nakit kod Srba, Beograd 1969.
       Trésors de l'art Serbe médiéval (XII - XVI siècle), Paris 1984.

Ristić, V   L'Eglise Lazarica et la place forte de Kruševac, Beograd 1989.

Skovran, A   Art in Medieval Serbia, Art Heritage of Serbia, Beograd 1984.

Steel, GS   The Medieval Monasteries of Serbia, Christian East. 1929.

Talbot-Rice, D   Byzantine Painting: The last phase, London 1968.
       The appreciation of Byzantine Art, London 1972.

Todić, B   Gračanica Slikarstvo, Beograd 1988.

Tomić, G   Jedna varijanta u okviru Moravske škole, Moravska škola i
       njeno doba. 1972.

Temperley, HWV History of Serbia, London: Bell 1912.

All these books are in the British Library Collection